# SEMINARY JOURNAL

Volume 22          Number One          Spring 2025

The *Seminary Journal* is a journal of opinion, research, and praxis in the field of seminary education and formation for priesthood within the Roman Catholic tradition. Articles are selected, edited, and published by the General Editor under the aegis of En Route Books and Media, LLC.

Dr. Sebastian Mahfood, OP, General Editor

**ISBN**: 979-8-88870-365-6

**Distribution Policy**

In recognition of limited staff and in light of changes in reader access preferences, articles submitted to *Seminary Journal* are normatively published online with the occasional print distribution.

**Subscriptions & Back Issues**

For the sake of universal access, all new issues of Seminary Journal are posted as PDFs online at https://www.seminaryjournal.com. Those interested in print copies may order them via Amazon.com through a link that will be provided on the website. By leveraging Amazon.com's fulfillment services, *Seminary Journal* avoids the expense of printing, warehousing, and shipping current and back copies, which means greater flexibility for creation and dissemination of each issue.

**E-Mail**:

contactus@enroutebooksandmedia.com

**Web site:**

https://www.seminaryjournal.com

**Call for Articles**

The *Seminary Journal* editors welcome articles related to seminary life, policy issues, and the priestly formation process. If you would like to submit an idea for an article or a document, please contact us.

Manuscripts should be submitted in Microsoft Word format and sent via e-mail attachment to En Route Books and Media at contactus@enroutebooksandmedia.com

**Guidelines**

The *Journal* guidelines are available at https://seminaryjournal.com/article-guidelines/

**Disclaimer**

Views expressed in the articles are those of the respective authors and not necessarily of *Seminary Journal* or of En Route Books and Media, LLC. The editors reserve the right to either reject submitted copy or edit it for clarity of presentation. All submissions accepted by the editors will go through a double-blind peer review process. If necessary, a document will be returned to the authors with recommendations for revisions.

**Index of *Seminary Journal***

For an online index of articles featured in *Seminary Journal* since 1995, please visit us online at http://www.seminaryjournal.com. Published by En Route Books and Media, LLC, 5705 Rhodes Avenue, St. Louis, MO 63109.

# SEMINARY JOURNAL

Volume 22        Number One        Spring 2025

## CONTENTS

# From the Desk of the General Editor

This edition of *Seminary Journal* is being published in the wake of the death of Pope Francis (1936-2025). His passing marks the end of an era—one shaped by bold compassion, pastoral outreach, and a renewed call to missionary discipleship.

At En Route Books and Media and WCAT Radio, his teachings and tone have not only guided us, but they have also inspired meaningful reflection and even respectful disagreement. During his pontificate, Pope Francis challenged the Church to "go to the peripheries," extending mercy and accompaniment to those on the margins. His pastoral vision deeply resonated in many of the works we've published and broadcasted.

But Pope Francis also invited rigorous thought, not blind allegiance, and many of our authors have examined areas where some felt his emphasis on pastoral sensitivity raised complex questions about doctrinal continuity. Our authors did not shy away from these questions—they explored them with reverence, always within the bounds of faithful Catholic inquiry.

On WCAT Radio, thousands of episodes aired since 2016 have reflected this wide spectrum: joyful support, critical engagement, and open-hearted discernment—mirroring Pope Francis's own encouragement of "honest dialogue" in the life of the Church.

Though his papacy sometimes stirred controversy, his heart was always with the people—and his witness has left an indelible mark. He has reminded us that doctrine without love is noise, and that mercy without truth is hollow.

For what comes next, En Route is poised to continue its work with a new generation of Catholic authors who will be formed during the upcoming papacy in light of our 2000-year tradition. We expect our work will continue to benefit programs of priestly and lay formation as directed by the 6th edition (2022) of the *Program of Priestly Formation* (*PPF*) and the upcoming successor document to the 2005 *Co-Workers in the Vineyard*. Our confidence in moving forward with so much that's new derives from our reliance on the history and tradition of our Catholic faith through a church founded by Jesus Christ.

We express gratitude for authors and editors like Fr. Dennis Billy, C.Ss.R., who designed this issue of *Seminary Journal* for the purpose of advancing the conversation on the direction seminary formation is heading as the 6th edition of the *PPF* is implemented among the major American seminaries. Included within it are articles concerning the intellectual, human, spiritual, and pastoral formation of seminarians authored by the theology faculty of St. Mary's Seminary and University in Baltimore, MD, the first Catholic seminary established in the United States in 1791.

Sebastian Mahfood, OP, Ph.D.
General Editor

# Introduction

In the Fall of 2023, the faculty of the School of Theology at St. Mary's Seminary & University in Roland Park, Baltimore, decided to embark on a second common faculty writing project in collaboration with *Seminary Journal*. The project was coordinated by Fr. Dennis Billy, C.Ss.R. The purpose of this effort on the part of the faculty was to encourage its members in light of the new *Ratio Fundamentalis* from Rome (2016) and the sixth edition of the *Program for Priestly Formation* (approved 2022) to delve more deeply into the various academic disciplines offered at the seminary, with an eye to how those disciplines should be taught in a Catholic seminary.

It was also hoped that such a project would encourage closer collaboration among the faculty, with the hope of seeing how these disciplines relate to one another and how classroom pedagogy has an impact on the content being both conveyed and received. Another hope was to offer the wider seminary community in the United States and beyond insights into how classroom pedagogy might impact the integration of the various dimensions of priestly formation.

Founded in 1791 by the Priests of Saint-Sulpice (the Sulpicians), St. Mary's Seminary is the oldest Catholic seminary in the United States and has prepared more men for priestly ordination than any other seminary in the United States. Animated by a core of dedicated Sulpician priests, the faculty consists of a unique blend of diocesan priests, religious, and laity, all of whom are dedicated to forming young men for the Catholic priesthood for the Church of the 21st century. It trains seminarians from more than ten dioceses as far apart as Portland, Maine and Richmond, Virginia and has rigorous standards for human, intellectual, and spiritual formation, spiritual direction, as well as pastoral outreach.

> "The purpose of this effort on the part of the faculty was to encourage its members . . . to delve more deeply into the various academic disciplines offered at the seminary, with an eye to how that discipline should be taught in a Catholic seminary."

In the end, eight faculty members participated in this common effort that ultimately produced eight individual essays on: theology as cultural witness; human formation in the twenty-first century; the diocesan priesthood and seminary formation; pastoral care and leadership in seminary formation; preparing foreign-born seminarians for the U.S. Church; political philosophy and Catholic social teaching; teaching Catholic history in seminary formation; and teaching Marian doctrine and spirituality in a Catholic seminary. Each faculty member was given free rein to develop the assigned essay as he or she saw fit (hence the different styles and approaches taken), the only exception being that it falls largely within the general guidelines of the journal. Although the areas presented do not exhaust the wide range of disciplines taught in Catholic seminaries, they represent a large portion of those offered and provide beginning reflections on how they should be integrated into the seminary program. It is hoped that this humble effort will encourage others to fill in the gaps with respect to those disciplines not treated in the present issue of the journal.

It should also be stated, although the entire faculty expressed interest in this common project, commitments of time and other responsibilities precluded everyone from participating in it.

That said, one way in which the faculty has gotten everyone involved was to use individual essays for topics of discussion during faculty development luncheons. Such a discussion format may be a way for other seminaries to benefit from the fruit of these essays.

The goal of this project was to strengthen the intellectual bonds within our own faculty and to offer insights into how the intellectual formation of Catholic seminarians could move forward in the years ahead. May this project encourage other faculties to contribute similar offerings to *Seminary Journal* in the years ahead.

Faculty
School of Theology
St. Mary's Seminary & University
Baltimore, Maryland

# Theology as Cultural Witness

## Barnabas Aspray, B.Sc., M.A., M.Phil., Ph.D., S.T.L.

Can theology offer a meaningful perspective on world events, one that guides us in how to understand and respond to the crises facing our time?

Before we answer this question, there is a question prior to it: *should* theology aim to do this? Does theology need to organize itself by popular topics and news headlines? Should theology not be concerned with preserving and passing on the mysteries of the faith: the Trinity, the Incarnation, Atonement, Justification by faith, Ecclesiology, sacraments, eschatology?

Well, yes, theology should be about those things. But if those things are only something one is "supposed to know" in order to count as a faithful Catholic – if the only interface they have with ordinary life is a set of inconvenient rules you have to keep – then those who leave the church cannot be blamed if they feel that it does not speak to their situation.

This article contends for the reframing of theology as "cultural witness," missional to the core. It is a *witness* to the truth of revelation, testifying to the core doctrines of the faith. It is *cultural* because it speaks *to* a particular culture *about* the questions and concerns of that culture, and how they are transformed and made clearer in the light of revelation. It is *missional* even when addressed to believers, because its aim should be to equip all believers, clergy and lay alike, to bring the light of truth into the dark confusion of the world.

This article proceeds in four steps. First, it dissociates the idea of cultural witness from the idea of "relevance" in theology. Turning instead to the idea of "illumination," it then characterizes theology as a light that can make the human condition and the world more intelligible. Thirdly, it argues that it is part of the essence of theology to be missional because it always has an implied addressee. Finally, it offers some practical and concrete resources as examples of cultural witness in the present day.

> **"This article contends for the reframing of theology as 'cultural witness,' missional to the core."**

## Should Theology be Relevant?

Theology does not need to be "relevant" to be true, nor is relevance the ultimate test for a doctrine's value. The pursuit of relevance can be dangerous and misleading, as is shown by the example of the doctrine of the Trinity. In the nineteenth century, Immanuel Kant criticized Trinitarian doctrine for having "no practical relevance at all."[1] In response to this, the twentieth-century movement known as "social Trinitarianism" sought to apply Trinitarian doctrine to human society, drawing lessons from their own speculations about the inner-Trinitarian life about how ecclesial or secular government should be organized, or about family dynamics. But the social Trinitarians' efforts were roundly criticized by Stephen Holmes and Karen Kilby (among others),[2] who exposed them as projections of the theologians' own political leanings, attributed to the Trinity and then reflected back on society with magnified authority as divinely mandated norms. The attempt to make the Trinity relevant only served to conflate Trinitarian doctrine with contemporary politics. Karen Kilby put it this way:

> Does the Trinity need to be relevant? What kind of relevance does it need to have? The doctrine of the Trinity arose in order to affirm certain things about the divinity of Christ, and, secondarily, of the Spirit, and it arose against a background assumption that God is one. So one could say that as long as Christians continue to believe in the divinity of Christ and the Spirit, and as long as they continue to believe that God is one, then the doctrine is alive and well; it continues to inform the way they read the Scriptures and the overall shape of their faith.[3]

Kilby saw that the "relevance" of Trinitarian doctrine is not found in its applicability to society or the church, but in its regulative function in keeping our focus on Jesus, on the Father, and on the Holy Spirit, the ultimate purpose, origin, and goal of our existence.

Nothing ages faster than relevance. What is relevant today is irrelevant tomorrow, so the quickest way to become obsolete is to get in tune with the current trends and fashions. The pursuit of relevance is also often a sign of shallowness, or a desperate need to appeal to the surrounding culture by making the church compete with shopping malls and movie theatres for the attention of the public. The church does not need to compete with the world. The church is not offering a product for sale, and its teachings do not need to be measured by the world's standards of usefulness or truth. Rather, theology is at its best when it draws from an agelong tradition, finding wisdom that has stood the test of time across countless cultures and ages.

On the other hand, theology is meant to illuminate the rest of life. St. Thomas Aquinas' famously defined theology as the study of God and all things in relation to God.[4] Not just sacred things: all things. That includes what we eat, what we wear, where we shop and go on vacation, what movies we watch, which car we drive, and how much time we spend on social media. It includes cars and candy, dogs and diapers, exercise and

[1] Immanuel Kant, *Religion and Rational Theology*, ed. and trans. Allen Wood and George Di Giovanni (Cambridge: Cambridge University Press, 2001), 264.
[2] Stephen R. Holmes, *The Quest for the Trinity: The Doctrine of God in Scripture, History and Modernity* (Downers Grove: IVP Academic, 2012); Karen Kilby, *God, Evil and the Limits of Theology* (Bloomsbury Publishing, 2020).
[3] Kilby, *God, Evil and the Limits of Theology*, 15.
[4] Thomas Aquinas, *ST* I, q. 1, a. 7.

entertainment. How is our study of Christ, the scriptures, the Church, and all the sacred mysteries informing and shaping our approach to those things?

If priests emerge from seminary knowing only about canon law, liturgical traditions, vestments, and other matters internal to the Church, then there is a danger they will have no wisdom to offer to parishioners who spend most of their time outside the Catholic bubble. They will be like people who know the answers to a quiz but don't know the questions. They possess the truth, but they have no idea why it's true or how its truth relates to world events. They will be standing at the center of a bubble, unable to show the meaningfulness of what they have learnt or communicate the faith effectively to those on the edge or outside it.

## The Illuminating Power of Theology

Theology's illuminating potential is expressed well by Étienne Gilson. Frustrated by the inward-looking nature of much Neo-Scholasticism, he wrote: "The modern Thomist is too often like someone holding a lamp, lost in the contemplation of its light and complaining that they see nothing. Let us only turn our light on the world of things around us, and we shall have plenty to see and to say."[5] The dogmas of the church were never meant to be objects whose purpose was to look at them, but a lens *through which* to view everything else in life. Today, the words "dogma" and "dogmatic" have connotations of stubborn inflexibility, refusal to dialogue, listen, or consider opposing viewpoints. Worse still, many Christians think of a dogma as something they are forbidden to doubt or question, as if it was a sin even to entertain the possibility that it is not true. That is how cults operate, but not the Church. Instead, we should recover the traditional sense of dogma as the DNA of any Christian worldview without which it is not authentically Christian. Of course, one may doubt or question it, but the word "dogma" makes clear that what one is doubting is Christianity in its essence, not some negotiable aspect of it.

In similar vein, René Latourelle criticized apologetic strategies that sought to prove the faith through brute-force logic, instead of by the illuminating power of its witness:

> After establishing by external arguments that Jesus is the messenger of God and that he founded a Church, classical apologetics concluded that we must receive from this Church everything that we are to believe. In drawing this conclusion, classical apologetics overlooked the fact (at least in practice) that the Christian message is supremely intelligible and that its very fullness of meaning is already a motive for accepting it in faith. Revelation is "believable" not only because of eternal signs but also because it reveals human beings to themselves; it is even the only key to an understanding of the mystery of the human person.[6]

---

[5] Étienne Gilson, *The Spirit of Thomism* (Washington, DC: Georgetown University Press, 1964), 93–94.

[6] René Latourelle, 'A New Image of Fundamental Theology', in *Problems and Perspectives of Fundamental*

Latourelle teaches us that the most effective

> **"*All* articles of faith can have the power to transform the way we see the world and understand ourselves if we only make the connection explicit."**

kind of apologetics is not that which provides compelling proofs of the articles of faith, but that which makes better sense of the human condition – daily life, politics, economics, relationships, and everything that human beings love, fear, need, and long for – than rival conceptions of reality. This accords with the kind of apologetics done by C.S. Lewis, who famously said: "I believe in Christianity as I believe that the sun has risen: not only because I see it but because by it I see everything else."[7] Likewise, Paul Ricœur saw his Christian faith as an asset to his philosophical writings, rather than an awkward obstacle to them. Drawing on Pascal, Ricœur wrote:

> I wager that I shall have a better understanding of man and of the bond between the being of man and the being of all beings if I follow the *indication* of [Christian anthropology]. … I bet at the same time *that* my wager will be restored to me in power of reflection, in the element of coherent discourse.[8]

But it is not only apologetics that needs to learn this lesson. *All* articles of faith can have the power to transform the way we see the world and understand ourselves if we only make the connection explicit. One of the most compelling features of any belief is whether or not it makes sense of the rest of reality. Many things are true, but not all true things are useful, giving wisdom to the one who believes them. There comes a moment when theology needs to prove its illuminating value by making *more* sense of the world we live in than any other belief system. If it can't do that, then this casts serious doubt on its truth.

## Missional Even When Addressed to Believers

"Today," writes Cardinal Raniero Cantalamessa, "the parable of the lost sheep is being lived out in reverse: ninety-nine sheep have gone away and only one has remained in the sheepfold. The danger is that we spend all our time nourishing the one remaining sheep."[9] The danger to which the Cardinal points is real, because it is easier to speak to fellow believers using a language, concepts, and a frame of reference we all share, than to go to the effort of building bridges of dialogue and mutual understanding with those outside the sheepfold.

However, when all the statistics confirm that people are leaving at a faster rate than they are

*Theology*, ed. René Latourelle and Gerald O'Collins, trans. Matthew J. O'Connell (New York: Paulist Press, 1982), 38.

[7] C.S. Lewis, *Essay Collection: Faith, Christianity and the Church* (HarperCollins UK, 2002), 21.

[8] Paul Ricœur, *The Symbolism of Evil*, trans. Emerson Buchanan (Boston: Beacon, 1969), 355. Italics original.

[9] Raniero Cantalamessa Cap OFM, *Shepherds and Fishermen: Spiritual Exercises for Bishops, Priests, and Religious* (Liturgical Press, 2020), 211.

joining, the New Evangelization need not only be about winning converts to the faith; it is also about preserving those already in the faith, so that the one sheep who remains does not give into the pressure to join the other ninety-nine. A layperson spends more than 90% of their time outside a church, where he or she is bombarded with messages from a worldview profoundly different to the Catholic one. The social environment of the Western world does not persuade people of its truth by logical or rational argument, but by addressing people at the level of their needs, desires, fears, longings, and hopes. It offers comfort, pleasure, safety, protection, guidance, and a way to happiness using a language and symbolism that makes sense to everyone who grew up in that social environment. If the Church is not doing the same, responding point by point to those same needs, desires, fears, longings, and hopes, then all it will have left to compel people is its appeal to a sense of moral duty and a fear of hell, a fear which will grow weaker as the plausibility of the Church's claims is slowly eroded by the crashing waves of

> **"When all the statistics confirm that people are leaving at a faster rate than they are joining, the New Evangelization need not only be about winning converts to the faith; it is also about preserving those already in the faith."**

the surrounding culture. How do we ensure that the faith remains compelling and plausible to people who were raised in it?

Perhaps it was with this question in mind that the Dominican friar Yves Congar wrote:

> If the Church wishes to deal with the real questions of the modern world and to attempt to respond to them, ... [then] instead of using only revelation and tradition as starting points, as classical theology has generally done, it must start with facts and questions derived from the world and from history.[10]

This statement – and similar ones by Jon Sobrino[11] – have frequently been misunderstood as rejecting the authoritative primacy of revelation and tradition. Surely revelation must be the starting point of any Christian thinking? But Congar and Sobrino do not mean by "starting point" to refer to an epistemological foundation for faith, as if the contemporary world's beliefs were a solid rock on which to build eternal truth. Rather, they meant that our exposition of the gospel should begin from where people currently are in their thinking, meeting them in their present condition instead of expecting them to come to where we are. Congar's point is not philosophical but pastoral, and it has nothing to do with altering the church's doctrines to suit the tastes of the culture. The starting point of mission and evangelism is not the same as the starting point of fundamental theology. The *philosophical* starting

---

[10] Cited in Gustavo Gutiérrez, *A Theology of Liberation,* trans. Sister Caridad Inda and John Eagleson (Orbis Books, 1988), 9–10.

[11] Jon Sobrino, *Christology at the Crossroads: A Latin American Approach* (Wipf and Stock Publishers, 2002).

point, better called the foundation, is not where anyone really starts; it is something achieved after laborious intellectual effort, working our way down to the foundations. Nobody encounters the gospel as a blank slate: every individual hears the gospel from a historical and cultural location, an existing language, social imaginary, worldview, and set of plausibility structures. The evangelistic starting point cannot be anywhere but there.

The culturally engaged nature of theology can be elucidated with the help of a key concept in philosophical hermeneutics. All discourse (whether textual, oral, or sign language) has the same structure: it is when *someone* (the author) says *something* (the text) to *someone* (the reader) about *something* (the subject matter). All four elements must be there for communication to occur. This means that communication is always to *someone*; it is never words uttered into the void. The implied addressee belongs to the essence of communication, and there is no communication without it. Theology cannot communicate itself to the outside world unless it takes into account the particular cultural framework of its addressees as part of its very self-expression.

## Where to Go from Here

Up until now, this article has been theorizing about theology as cultural witness. But what does this look like in practice? Are there any concrete examples of it going on?

Undoubtedly there are countless examples of effective cultural witness that I am not aware of. I will point to some recent initiatives that I know about because I am involved with them. All are ecumenical projects with participants from multiple Christian confessions – Anglican, Catholic, Reformed, Evangelical and others. Their ecumenical nature has some drawbacks, because they cannot speak boldly and authoritatively about topics on which Christians are divided. Nonetheless, they serve to show the power of what C.S. Lewis called "mere Christianity" – that the raw basics of Christianity still have enough distinctiveness to speak prophetically to the world and call it to account.

The Centre for Faith & Society, based at the University of Fribourg, Switzerland, is producing high-quality audio and video resources that critically analyze modern ways of thinking by asking penetrating questions about the underlying anthropological presuppositions that are operative.[12] One of their projects, "Contesting Computer Anthropologies,"[13] seeks to expose the ways we increasingly imagine human beings along the lines of a computer, with detrimental consequences. In the face of Artificial Intelligence that many feel as a threat, it proposes to restore a theological vision of human nature by pointing to all the things that make human

---

[12] 'Home | Center Faith & Society | University of Fribourg', accessed 12 November 2024, https://www.unifr.ch/glaubeundgesellschaft/en/.

[13] 'Contesting Computer Anthropologies', accessed 12 November 2024, https://www.unifr.ch/glaubeundgesellschaft/en/research/projects/cca.html.

beings distinctively human. Another project, "The End of Humanity?" addresses the contemporary transhumanist movement, comparing its vision of heaven, hell, and salvation to the vision given by Dante in *The Divine Comedy*.[14] The theological method behind these enterprises has been explicated in a special issue of *Religions Journal* dedicated to the concept of cultural witness.[15]

The Centre for Cultural Witness, based at Lambeth Palace Library, London, United Kingdom, was founded by (Anglican) Bishop Graham Tomlin with the goal of re-enchanting secular society with the message of the gospel.[16] They have a magazine, *Seen & Unseen*, drawn from a line in the creed about God the creator of all things "seen and unseen" (or visible and invisible).[17] The magazine's purpose is to make sense of the "seen" (the world and society) in light of the "unseen" (God, revelation, the supernatural claims of the Christian faith). All of its authors, of whom I am one,[18] write with a non-Christian audience in mind aiming to offer "Christian perspectives on just about everything." Although it does have some articles about Christianity itself, much of its content offers a "Christian take" on news, entertainment, and current events – things, in other words, that an unbeliever would be interested in. They also have a podcast and YouTube channel, called "The Re-Enchanting Podcast" in which they interview high-profile public figures, both believers and unbelievers, discussing the role that Christianity plays in today's Western society.[19]

Finally, I am the founder and co-host of a podcast, Faith at the Frontiers, that aims to "confront challenges to the Christian faith with hope." In each episode, I and my co-host interview a world expert on a "global challenge" – climate change, immigration, faith & science, colonialism, religious violence, the crusades, the Inquisition – and fearlessly ask the harder questions about whether these things discredit the Christian faith. The goal is not to engage in defensive apologetics, but to ask what Christians

> **"The goal of seminary training should be to produce priests who understand the modern world better than anyone else, not priests who give the impression that they are isolated from it."**

---

[14] 'The End of Humanity – We Need 100% of Humanity, Not 100% Automation.', accessed 12 November 2024, https://endofhumanity.film/.

[15] Christine Schliesser et al., eds., *Churches in Europe and the Challenge of Cultural Witness* (MDPI, 2023), https://www.mdpi.com/books/reprint/7988-churches-in-europe-and-the-challenge-of-cultural-witness.

[16] 'Centre for Cultural Witness', Centre for Cultural Witness, accessed 12 November 2024, https://www.culturalwitness.org.

[17] 'Seen & Unseen | Seen & Unseen', accessed 12 November 2024, https://www.seenandunseen.com/.

[18] 'Barnabas Aspray | Seen & Unseen', 13 September 2024, https://www.seenandunseen.com/contributors/barnabas-aspray.

[19] 'Re-Enchanting', Apple Podcasts, accessed 12 November 2024, https://podcasts.apple.com/us/podcast/re-enchanting/id1682867001; 'Seen & Unseen - YouTube', accessed 12 November 2024, https://www.youtube.com/@SeenUnseenMag.

can learn from these difficult topics that many would prefer to avoid thinking about.[20]

The goal of seminary training should be to produce priests who understand the modern world better than anyone else, not priests who give the impression that they are isolated from it. It is possible to make theology speak to the present day without sacrificing its depth and distinctiveness. Possible, but not easy. Not only possible, but essential. Yet it is never finally achieved. Drawing connection points between the dogmas of the faith and the society people actually live in and encounter day-in, day-out, is a never-ending task, begun anew with each new individual we encounter.

The Art of Accompaniment

Practical Steps for the Pastoral Mentor

Sr. Marysia Weber, RSM, DO, MA

Barnabas Aspray, B.Sc., M.A., M.Phil., Ph.D., S.T.L.
(baspray@stmarys.edu)

Dr. Aspray is Assistant Professor of Systematic Theology at St. Mary's Seminary & University.

This book presents an integral approach to formation during the vocational synthesis stage, weaving together the human, spiritual, intellectual, and pastoral dimensions of priestly preparation. It is responsive to the Church's vision articulated in *Pastores Dabo Vobis*, *Ratio Fundamentalis*, and the *Program of Priestly Formation* (6th edition), offering formators a comprehensive framework for accompanying transitional deacons in their final preparation for priesthood. By providing formators with both a synthetic vision of integral formation and practical tools for implementation, it enables mentors to accompany transitional deacons through the vital process of vocational synthesis, helping them integrate their years of formation into a coherent priestly identity. May this work be for God's glory and the good of His devoted servants.

Only $14.95. Available with a free template for benchmarks online at https://enroutebooksandmedia.com/practicalsteps/

---

[20] 'Faith at the Frontiers', Faith at the Frontiers, accessed 12 November 2024, https://faithatthefrontiers.com.

# Human Formation in the Twenty-first Century

**Phillip Brown, P.S.S., J.D., J.C.D.**

*Every high priest is taken from among men and made their representative before God, to offer gifts and sacrifices for sins. He is able to deal patiently with the ignorant and erring, for he himself is beset by weakness.*

Hebrews 5: 1-2

## Introduction

"The whole work of priestly formation would be deprived of its necessary foundation if it lacked a suitable human formation."[1] A priest is a human being before he is a priest. Before he was a seminarian, he was a young man, or an older man, living the ongoing process of human growth and development. At whatever stage of that process, every seminarian has a way to go toward greater maturity, self-possession, self-discipline, and the ongoing cultivation of those human qualities that will make him more effective in human interactions and as a priest and pastor.

> **"Human formation is directed toward helping others promote their own growth, development, and human flourishing."**

---

[1] Eighth Ordinary General Assembly - The Formation of Priests in Circumstances of the Present Day (30 September-28 October 1990), *Proposition 8.*

## Christian Anthropology and Human Formation

Christian anthropology holds that all human beings are flawed, suffering the consequences of that primeval fault we call Original Sin. "Every priest is taken from among men ... he is able to deal patiently with the ignorant and erring, for he himself is beset by weakness." The starting point for human formation is the human reality of fallen human nature in need of redemption, healing, development, and maturation; a lifelong process; a dynamic process of growth and development, maturation, and the remediation of deficits that every human being suffers from. With respect to candidates for the priesthood, it is a process regarding one's personality, character, and capacity to relate with other human beings. Human formation is directed toward helping others promote their own growth, development, and human flourishing. Priests choose a way of life that is dedicated to serving God and the Church, and the human and spiritual flourishing of others; to serving their spiritual and incarnate well-being; to helping them achieve good health and wholeness, that is towards their salvation. As a priest, he is able to deal patiently with flawed and wounded human beings because he knows he himself is flawed, wounded, and in need of healing. And in promoting the healing, wellbeing, and integrity of others, he promotes and achieves his own.

The human dimension of seminary formation gets the process of healing and human flourishing going and seeks to assure that it will continue. The goal is that when a seminarian graduates and goes on to priestly ordination his seminary formators will be able to say with confidence, "Will the one who began this good work in you continue to complete it right up until the day of Christ Jesus."[2]

## Foundations of Human Formation

"Human formation" is not something new in the education and training of priests. It has been of concern from the earliest times of the institutional Church, even if spoken of differently in earlier times. With the advent of psychology and the behavioral sciences as a primary lens through which human growth, development and flourishing are viewed today, we speak of the underlying issues in different ways. But the basic issues of human development and character remain the same. The early Church was heir to classical traditions about what makes for a healthy, well-functioning human being. In that tradition, the

requisite human qualities were discussed in terms of the acquisition and cultivation of "virtues" and "character", general terms which sought to express those human qualities considered desirable for functioning well in society and contributing to its wellbeing. In the Church, these concepts came to be applied to priests and those preparing to be priests. As early as the late 380's St. Ambrose of Milan produced a treatise on the duties of clergy, *De Officiis Ministrorum*, much of which describes the desired qualities of sacred ministers in terms of that classical tradition.[3]

Those involved in human formation

> "Those involved in human formation work in seminaries today can benefit from becoming familiar with these traditional points of view on the human qualities required to be an effective sacred minister."

work in seminaries today can benefit from becoming familiar with these traditional points of view on the human qualities required to be an effective sacred minister, especially when considered in the context of contemporary viewpoints derived from the relevant human sciences as they have developed over the past two hundred years or so. The classic model, which focused on identifiable "virtues" and what was referred to as "character", remain valid and are still referred to

---

[2] Philippians 1:6.

[3] St. Ambrose of Milan, *De Officiis*, Edited with an Introduction, Translation, and Commentary by Ivor J. Davidson, Oxford University Press, The Oxford Early Christian Studies Series, (Oxford, 2001).

in Church literature regarding formation. But they must be interpreted in the light of the contemporary world, contemporary behavioral expectations in general, and ecclesial behavioral expectations in particular. By studying both ancient and modern sources regarding the formation of desirable human qualities for the exercise of sacred ministry, formators will be well-equipped to work with the seminarians of today in nurturing the qualities necessary for effective pastoral ministry and a satisfying and enriching life as a priest.

The following works are valuable for tracing the history of the Church's outlook on human formation to put it into a contemporary context: St. Ambrose of Milan, *De Officiis*; St. Alphonsus Ligouri, *The Dignity and Duties of the Priest*; Fr. J. B. Hogan, S.S., *Clerical Studies*; studies commission by the USCCB in the late 1960's under the title *The Catholic Priest in the United States*; the developmental theories of the Swiss psychologist Jean Piaget, and the American psychologist Abraham Maslow; and a recent study by the American social psychologist Jonathan Haidt entitled *The Anxious Generation*.

## Background Resources

### St. Ambrose: *De Officiis*

St. Ambrose of Milan proposed an ideal for the attitude and behavior of priests in his treatise *De Officiis*. He grounded this ideal on his conception of the dignity of ministerial offices in the Church. He set the tone for the way offices of ministry in the Church would be viewed ever

since. As a diocesan Bishop, he exhorted his priests to reflect the dignity of their vocation both for their own wellbeing and as an

> "By studying both ancient and modern sources regarding the formation of desirable human qualities for the exercise of sacred ministry, formators will be well-equipped to work with the seminarians of today in nurturing the qualities necessary for effective pastoral ministry and a satisfying and enriching life as a priest."

example of how to live the Christian life for those they served. He took as his model a similar treatise, also entitled *De Officiis*, by the Roman statesman, orator, and writer on philosophy Cicero concerning the duties and manner of living of a Roman gentleman. Ambrose relied on Roman ideals of gentlemanliness and service, which he summed up in the term *decorum*, to provide the Church with an ideal for the attitudes and behavior of the Church's ministers. He adopted Roman traditions regarding what is right, becoming, and honorable (*decorum*), and went on to consider also what is expedient (*utile*). He applied these concepts to virtuous conduct in this life, but also towards attainment of the life to come.

In the first book of his treatise, Ambrose discusses the ordinary duties that all are bound to (such as toward one's parents and elders), and then those that go beyond fulfilling obligations by which one strives for perfection, an idealistic goal. He proposes that two principles lead the mind: reason and appetite. What is decorous consists in thinking first about good and right things, and then subjecting the appetites to reason. He ends with a consideration of the four cardinal virtues of prudence, justice, fortitude, and temperance.[4]

While promoting an exalted view of the dignity of sacred orders and ministerial offices, Ambrose nevertheless considered this dignity in the context of the human reality of real men. He emphasizes cultivating the classic virtues as the foundation for acquiring *decorum*, that is a well-integrated personality and manner of interacting with others that reflects a decorous attitude and decorous habits, understood according to the classical model of the "virtuous person".

Ambrose's treatise had a major influence on Church culture, clerical culture in particular, which can still be seen in the ideals of clerical attitudes and behavior, especially in its upper echelons. Understanding Ambrose's ideal is valuable background for reflecting upon how to incorporate the best of those ideals into the formation of priests with a well-integrated and pleasing personality, capable of relating well to others, today for the sake of promoting effective pastoral ministry and a satisfying priestly way of life. Ambrose's *De Officiis* is, therefore, foundational for understanding the further development of his

ideal in later works, such as St. Alphonsus Ligouri's *Dignity and Duties of the Priest*.

## St. Alphonsus Liguori: *Dignity and duties of the Priest*

St. Alphonsus Ligouri had a very exalted view of the priesthood: "I am a priest; my dignity is above that of the angels. I should then lead a life of angelic purity, and I am obliged to strive for this by all possible means."[5]

*Dignity and Duties of the Priest* contains materials prepared by St. Alphonsus for giving retreats to priests, for developing a rule of life, and spiritual rules to guide priests in their day-to-day lives. His ideas are valuable for understanding the history and context of views of the priesthood within the Catholic Church, even if at times they may seem anachronistic and too idealistic. Young men tend to be idealistic nonetheless, however. Emphasizing the exalted station of the priest is often appealing to them, but when excessive can promote a negative kind of clericalism. It is important, therefore, to moderate overly exalted views of the priesthood, rather than reinforce them.

Men who become priests need to be aware of the kind of real spiritual and temporal power and responsibilities conferred on them by ordination, and that they do play a unique role in the life and

[4] New Advent, Introduction to "On the Duties of the Clergy", transl. by H. de Romestin, E. de Romestin and H.T.F. Duckworth. From *Nicene and Post-Nicene Fathers, Second Series*, Vol. 10, ed. Philip Schaff and Henry Wace, (Buffalo, NY: Christian Literature Publishing Co., 1896.), revised and edited for New Advent by Kevin Knight <http://www.newadvent.org/fathers/34011.htm>

[5] St. Alphonsus Ligouri, *Dignity and Duties of the Priest; or Selva*, ed. Eugene Grimm, Benzinger Brothers (New York, Cincinnati, Chicago 1889), p. 9.

administration of the Church. It's a matter of striking the proper balance between the exalted station of the priesthood and the imperative that priests be humble to be able to serve worthily. Achieving that balance concerns both human and spiritual formation. As Pope St. Paul II acknowledged in *PDV*, however, formation has to begin with the human person, the human qualities of candidates from a natural standpoint, as the necessary foundation for the successful cultivation of a priestly spiritual life and behaviors.

St. Alphonsus composed fifteen "resolutions" when he was approved for ordination to the priesthood, which reveal his high idealism but also represent worthy goals for a priestly demeanor when considered in context:

1. I am a priest; my dignity is above that of the angels. I should then lead a life of angelic purity, and I am obliged to strive for this by all possible means.

2. A God deigns to obey my voice. I should, with far greater reason, obey his speaking to me through his inspirations or my Superiors.

2. The holy Church has honored me: I must therefore honor myself by sanctity of life, by my zeal and labors, etc.

4. I offer to the Eternal Father Jesus Christ, his Son; it is then my duty to

clothe myself with the virtues of Jesus Christ, that I may become fit for my office.

5. Christian people see in me a minister of reconciliation, a mediator between God and man; consequently, I must always keep myself in the grace and friendship of God.

6. The faithful desire to see in me a model of the virtues to which they should aspire; I must then be edifying always and under all circumstances.

7. Poor sinners that have lost the light of grace come to me to be spiritually resuscitated: I must therefore aid them by my prayers, exhortations, and good example.

8. Courage is necessary to triumph over the world, the flesh, and the devil; I must then correspond with divine grace that I may combat these virtues victoriously.

9. To defend religion and fight against error and impiety, one must have knowledge. I will then strive, by every means within my reach, to acquire the necessary knowledge.

10. Human respect and worldly friendships dishonor the priesthood; I will then avoid them.

11. Ambition and self-interest have often caused priests to lose their faith; I must then abhor these vices as sources of reprobation.

12. Gravity should accompany charity in a priest; I will then be prudent and reserved, especially with regard to women, without being proud, rough, or disdainful.

13. I can please God only by recollection, fervor, and solid virtue, which nourish the holy exercise of prayer; I will then neglect nothing which may tend to their acquisition.

14. I should seek only the glory of God, my own sanctification, and the salvation of souls; consequently, I must achieve these ends though it should cost my life.

15. I am a priest; it is my duty to inspire virtue in all with whom I come in contact, and to glorify Jesus Christ, the eternal High-priest.[6]

St. Alphonsus also wrote twelve "rules of conduct" for himself while still in the seminary, which interpreted in the light of contemporary culture remain valid ideals for human and spiritual formation:

1. The cleric should frequent the society of holy priests, to be edified by their example.

2. He should spend at least one hour daily in mental prayer so that he may live in fervor and recollection.

3. He should visit the Blessed Sacrament frequently, especially during the time of exposition.

4. He should read the lives of holy priests that he may imitate their virtues

5. He must cultivate a special devotion to the Holy Virgin, the Mother and Queen of the clergy, and consecrate himself particularly to her service.

6. For the honor of the ecclesiastical state he must be most careful of his reputation.

---

[6] Ibid., pp. 9-11.

7. He should flee from worldly conversation, and not be too familiar with the laity, especially women.

8. Seeing God in his Superiors, he must obey them, because such is the divine will.

9. He should be modest, but without affectation, severity, or fastidiousness; and he should always wear the cassock and tonsure.

10. He should be quiet and gentle at home, exemplary in class, and edifying in church, especially during the public offices.

11. He should confess every eight days and communicate still oftener.

12. He should live free from sin and practice every virtue.

## Modern Era

## Recourse to the behavioral sciences

St. Ambrose and St. Alphonsus can be seen as setting out the "classical" view of the objectives of human formation based on the ideas of virtue, character, and decorum. Starting in the late nineteenth century, those involved in seminary formation began advocating for greater incorporation of the natural sciences in seminary curricula and recourse to the insights of the behavioral sciences, especially psychology, in seminary formation programs. This represented a shift of emphasis from an idealistic view of the priesthood to a realistic appraisal of what is humanly possible in cultivating the ideals of a priestly way of life, with particular emphasis on the study of human development and developmental psychology. One could say that this more modern view considers every human being as a "work in progress" throughout life, and that seldom does anyone

> "This more modern view considers every human being as a "work in progress" throughout life."

achieve the highest ideals of maturity, demeanor, or behavior. The outlook of formators has therefore shifted to considerations of how to support human growth and development, and the maturation process, while not placing unrealistic expectations on either seminarians or priests.

In the late nineteenth century Sulpician Rector and scholar J. B. Hogan, President of St. John's Seminary in Brighton, Massachusetts, advocated for the inclusion of natural sciences in seminary curricula and recourse to the behavioral sciences for understanding better how to form the character of candidates for the priesthood and help them develop virtuous ways of living. The Bishops Conference of the U.S. set seminary programs on a trajectory of full incorporation of the insights of the behavioral sciences in priestly formation in 1967, authorizing "a complete, professional, and objective study of the life and ministry of priests"[7] to be done from several different perspectives (historical, sociological, psychological, etc.). According to the Forward to the first volume of the study, "The bishops of the United States were eager to learn the precise nature and dimensions of the difficulties experienced by priests as a result of the radical and rapid social and moral changes in contemporary life."[8]

Some aspects of the studies are controversial, but the data they contain is valid and of ongoing interest, providing context for the development of human formation programs today. Attention to scientific perspectives has, if anything, become even more urgent in light of what has been learned over the past forty years in relation to the sexual abuse of minors and other misconduct by priests and other church ministers.[9] The psychological characteristics and sociological context of men entering the seminary today may differ from 1967, but the analytical methodology and general insights offered by the USCCB studies continue to be relevant and provide useful templates for considering these issues.

Kennedy and Heckler, who studied the priesthood from the perspective of psychology, found in the late 1960s that the personal characteristics and life satisfaction of priests and seminarians were, in general, similar if not identical to men in other demographic groups. They concluded:

The priests of the United States are ordinary men. Many of their conflicts and challenges arise precisely because they are ordinary men who may have to live as though they were not ordinary at all. Perhaps no group of men has such high expectations placed on it by the Church, society, themselves and even their closest personal associates. Psychoanalyst Margaretta K. Bowers (1963) has written that "all through the ages the clergy have suffered from the insurmountable contrast between their very real humanity and the transcendent requirement of their symbolic representation as the priest, the Incarnate Christ".[10]

Kennedy and Heckler also concluded, "Speaking in summary terms again, American priests are bright and good men who do not as a group suffer from major psychological problems".[11] They did feel a large number of the priests of their day were underdeveloped as persons, with a consequent lack of fully realized religious and human values in their lives," but also that "They are not sick; they are not fully grown … The priests of the United States are clearly

[7] *The Catholic Priest in the United States: Historical Investigations*, ed., John Tracy Ellis, Saint John's University Press (Collegeville, MN 1071), Forward, pl; vii.

[8] Ibid.

[9] See, in particular: John Jay College of Criminal Justice (2004), "Executive Summary" (PDF), *The Nature and Scope of Sexual Abuse of Minors by Catholic Priests and Deacons in the United States 1950–2002*, United States Conference of Catholic Bishops, ISBN 1-57455-627-4,

[10] Eugene C. Kennedy, M.M., Ph.D. and Victor J. Heckler, Ph.D., *The Catholic Priest in the United States: Psychological Investigations*, Washington, D.C. (United States Catholic Conference, 1972), p. 3.

[11] Ibid.

adequate in their function, they could be far more effective personally and professionally if they were helped to achieve greater human and religious maturity."[12]

Eugene C. Kennedy went on to become a well-known figure in the Catholic world who left the priesthood and married. He consistently said that he supported celibacy for Catholic priests but advocated that it be optional, not mandatory. This should be taken into consideration when relying on his interpretations, given that celibacy has not become optional for Catholic priests but continues to be mandatory.

The conclusions in the USCCB study were not unlike those of the priest psychiatrist Steven Rossetti forty years later in his extensive study of the priesthood *Why Priests are Happy: A Study of the Psychological and Spiritual Health of Priests.*[13] The lesson for formators concerned with the human formation of candidates for the priesthood today would seem to be to develop programs that assure that candidates leave the seminary capable of fully realizing religious and human values in their lives.

### Pastores Dabo Vobis

In 1990, the Synod of Bishops took as its principal theme *The Formation of Priests in the Circumstances of the Present Day*, resulting in Pope St. John Paul II's Post-Synodal Apostolic Exhortation *Pastores dabo vobis* (*PDV*) which set forth proposals, guidance, and norms for seminary formation programs which served as the primary source of such guidance from 1992 until promulgation of the 2016 *Ratio fundamentalis institutionis sacerdotalis.*

Paragraph 43 of *PDV* refers to human formation as the "necessary foundation" of all formation for the priesthood. John Paul II summarizes and synthesizes developments pertaining to human formation from the classical approach through the more recent focus on the behavioral sciences, outlining his vision of human formation as follows (footnotes omitted):

93. The divine call engages and involves the 'concrete' human person. Formation for the priesthood must . . . allow for maturation in view of . . . authentic priestly ministry . . . the seminarian is called upon to develop his personality, having Christ, the perfect man, as his model and source.

. . . A correct and harmonious spirituality demands a well-structured humanity; . . . as St. Thomas Aquinas reminds us, "*grace builds upon nature*", it does not supplant nature, but perfects it. Therefore, it is necessary to cultivate humility, courage, common sense, magnanimity,

---

[12] Ibid., p. 16.

[13] Stephen J. Rossetti, *Why Priests are Happy: A Study of Psychological and Spiritual Health of Priests.* Notre Dame, Indiana (Ave Maria Press, 2011), pp. 237.

right judgement and discretion, tolerance and transparency, love of truth and honesty.

94. Human formation, being the foundation of all priestly formation, promotes the integral growth of the person and allows the integration of all its dimensions. Physically, this means an interest in health, nutrition, physical activity, and rest; psychologically it focuses on the constitution of a stable personality, characterized by emotional balance, self-control and a well-integrated sexuality. In the moral sphere, it is connected to the requirement that the individual arrive gradually at a well-formed conscience. This means that he will become a responsible person able to make the right decisions, gifted with right judgement, and able to have an objective perception of persons and events. Such a perspective should bring the seminarian to a balanced sense of self respect, leading him to be aware of his own talents and learning how to place them at the service of the People of God. The aesthetic sense should also be cultivated in human formation, by offering opportunities for an appreciation of various modes of artistic expression, cultivating in him the 'sense of beauty'. He ought to be aware of the social environment and be helped to improve his capacity for social interaction so that he can contribute to building up the community in which he lives.

In order for this training to be fruitful, it is important that every seminarian be aware of his own life history and be ready to share it with his formators. This would include especially his experience of childhood and adolescence, the influence that his family and his relatives have exercised upon him, his ability to establish mature and well-balanced interpersonal relationships, or his lack thereof, and his ability to handle positively moments of solitude. Such information will be helpful for choosing the most fitting pedagogical means, both for an assessment of the journey thus far and for a better understanding of any moments of regression or of difficulty.

95. A sign of the harmonious development of the personality of seminarians is a mature capacity for relations with men and women of various ages and social conditions.

## The 2016 *Ratio fundamentalis* and *PPF6*

The 1971 *Ratio fundamentalis insitutionis sacerdotalis* was revised, and a new *Ratio* promulgated in 2016. This, in turn, led to the completion of the *Sixth Edition* of the *Program for*

*Priestly Formation* for the United States in 2022. The new *Ratio* significantly re-structures the *process* of priestly formation, but restates in substance, if not literally, the principles of *PDV* regarding human formation referred to above, with a couple of additional observations pertinent to today's context:

99. Those who begin the Seminary journey are, for the most part, already naturally quite adept and immersed in the digital world and its instruments. It is necessary to pay prudent attention to the inevitable risks that come with frequenting the digital world, including various forms of addiction, which can be addressed with suitable spiritual and psychological supports.

. . .

100. Social [media] networks should be integrated into the daily life of the Seminary community in a particular way (by a use that is vigilant, but also serene and positive). They should be experienced as places that offer new possibilities from the point of view of interpersonal relationships, of encounter with others, of engagement with one's neighbor, of the witness of faith. These may all be viewed from the perspective of formative growth, which cannot fail to take into consideration every place in which relationships are formed and in which we find ourselves living.

Two major considerations formators need to attend to in the twenty-first century remain what they have been in recent decades: contemporary views of the human person that are not consonant with a Christian anthropology; and the adaptation of concepts and techniques of human formation to the ever-evolving social context that seminary candidates come to the seminary from. One of those social developments that has had a tremendous impact on those entering the seminary today, with important implications for their human formation, is the impact of social media and other digitally-based technologies on entering seminarians deriving from the technological revolution occurring since the 1990's. The influences of the social media culture on entering seminarians ought to be of special concern to seminary formators today and is addressed below. Evidence has now been compiled that verifies the significant impact these developments

> "Two major considerations formators need to attend to in the twenty-first century remain what they have been in recent decades: con-temporary views of the human person that are not consonant with a Christian anthropology; and the adaptation of concepts and techniques of human formation to the ever-evolving social context that seminary candidates come to the seminary from."

have had on the psychology and socialization of young people during the past decade, in ways that it can be argued have significantly altered their way of perceiving and experiencing the world around them, and their own sense of identity and social adaptation, in comparison with previous generations. Formators cannot assume that seminarians today have experienced the world in the same way they have, nor that they can always easily or immediately understand the perceptual and inner worlds of these seminarians.

## USCCB *PPF6*

The 2022 *PPF6* of the USCCB also follows closely the principles and norms of the *Ratio* and *PDV*. It asserts first of all that the foundation and center of all human formation is the Word made flesh (¶181), and goes on to repeat that "The basic principle of human formation is found in Pastores Dabo Vobis: the human personality of the priest is to be a bridge and not an obstacle for others in their meeting with Jesus Christ, the Redeemer of the human race (¶182)," repeating then all of the virtues and character based traits outlined in PDV and the cautions of the *Ratio* regarding digital technology and social media (¶¶183-186). It goes on to outline human formation "benchmarks" that ought to be reached at each stage of formation for candidates to advance to the next level or to receive a positive recommendation for Holy Orders.

## An anxious generation?

Given the concerns raised in the *Ratio* and *PPF6* regarding digital technology and social media, a useful and important resource for seminary formators concerned with human formation, which the author recommends, is *The Anxious Generation* by the American social psychologist Jonathan Haidt.[14] Haidt catalogs accumulating data demonstrating that the emergence of digital technology and social media has had a significant impact on the psychology and cognitive perception of young people in the Anglophone world from about 2010 onward (paralleling the appearance of widely available and utilized social media). Although not a product of digital technology and social media in and of themselves, the manner in which social media has been "marketed" by social media companies has exacerbated negative effects inherent in human psychology and social adaptation in relation to social media use. The impact of these dynamics on adolescent psychology in young people since 2010 is striking and undeniable. Major depression among teens has skyrocketed since 2010, exactly paralleling rising rates of social media use by young people. Major depression has risen 145% among young girls and 161% among boys between 2010 and 2024.[15] Among college students, anxiety has risen by 134%, depression 106%, ADHD 72%, bipolar disorder 57%, Anorexia 100%, substance abuse or addiction 33%, and

---

[14] Jonathan Haidt, *The Anxious Generation*, Penguin Press (New York, 2024).

[15] Ibid., 24.

schizophrenia 67%. The highest rate of increase has been in young people ages 18-25 (139%), with those 26-34 experiencing a 103% increase, 35-49 a 52% increase, and with those 50 or older experiencing only negligible increases. This mental health crisis has, therefore, predominantly been affecting young people, those age groups entering seminarians come from. The impact of these factors and the importance of being aware of them and being prepared to address them in seminary formation programs is therefore evident and urgent. Further documented impacts have been a 188% increase in emergency room visits for self-harm among girls and a 48% increase among boys. Suicide rates have risen 91% among boys and 161% among girls during the same period.

Haidt analyzes the psychological and sociological dynamics involved in social media marketing and use, which he argues suggest how they have conditioned young people growing up during at least the past fifteen years in ways that have resulted in the meteoric rise in mental health and other problems among them. Seminary formators have to assume that candidates coming to their programs will exhibit the same mental health and behavioral challenges faced by other young people of their generation, given the generalized nature of the problems identified by the data Haidt relies on, which one has every reason to believe is reliable. Formators must therefore acquaint themselves with this data and the underlying causes of the problems they reveal in order to develop programs and approaches to formation that will help the seminarians they are

forming to recognize the mental health and behavioral issues that have become a part of the life experience of members of their generation, and how those issues can be addressed successfully. Their human formation and ability to acquire the kind of sound and stable mental, emotional, and behavioral stability, and good health necessary to become effective ministers of the Gospel and pastors will depend on this, not to mention in order for them to be able to live out their vocations in a way that will be enriching and satisfying, humanly as well as spiritually and pastorally. It will be difficult for men in the seminary today to serve effectively as priests and pastors without first undergoing the kind of healing and maturation Haidt's data and analysis suggest is needed by virtually all members of the generation that has grown up conditioned by the dynamics he exposes in his research.

Haidt identifies a number of psychological and sociological phenomena that have fueled the negative dynamics unleashed by the social media era, and that have conditioned young people towards the kind of negative mental health and behavioral results his data identifies, an understanding of which by formators will be very useful for better understanding the young men entering the seminary today and how to support their human formation and maturation while they are in the seminary. Those who are in charge of human formation are, therefore, encouraged to become familiar with these concepts by studying Haidt's findings and other resources for addressing this current phenomenon.

Formators may recognize the characteristics Haidt describes but not understand where they have come from, or how powerful they have been in conditioning the perceptions and behavior of the young people who have been subjected to them, how to name them in order to gain a deeper understanding of what they are and how they operate, and what can be done to address them in ways that will lead to better mental health, self-possession, and the kind of maturity expected of seminarians who are now adults and candidates for leadership positions in the Christian community as priests. Haidt explains the psychological dynamics of what he refers to as *conformist bias* and *prestige bias* that are such a significant part of the social media phenomenon, and that social media companies have, in fact, exploited in order to achieve their aggressive marketing objectives. Haidt states that "Social media platforms are . . . the most efficient conformity engines ever invented. They can shape an adolescent's mental models of acceptable behavior in a matter of hours. Parents . . . are often no match for the socializing power of social media."[16] Much less seminary formators, if they are not well-equipped to understand and address these dynamics when they produce results contrary to the attitudes and behavior that seminary formation is endeavoring to inculcate.

*Conformist bias* is not difficult to understand: It means that human beings have a natural tendency to do whatever most people are doing as the safest strategy across a wide range of environments. It's nothing new in human behavior. What has changed is the power of social media to define and influence those who use it regularly to behave in the ways that social media creates the perception is what most people are doing and thinking. One of the most powerful ways it accomplishes this is through *prestige bias*. People are not only influenced to do what *most* people are doing, they are even more powerfully influenced to mimic those they perceive as prestigious. Human beings are hardwired, as they say, to "detect prestige and then copy the prestigious".[17] Hence the rise of social media "influencers": Those who create an aura of prestige and then communicate their views of what is acceptable and desirable in beliefs and behavior. Millions upon millions of social media users then adopt those beliefs and behave in those ways, influenced by *prestige bias*. The extent to which seminarians today have used social media is a significant factor, along with an assessment of how easily they are influenced by social media, and their capacity to exercise critical thinking skills in assessing social media content and other kinds of information they have recourse to, and the strength of their capacity for independent thinking. "TikTok's own research notes that, for teenagers, 'compulsive usage correlates with a slew of negative mental health effects like loss of analytical skills, memory formation, contextual thinking, conversational depth, empathy, and

---

[16] Ibid. 59.

[17] Ibid., 60.

increased anxiety.'"[18] These are significant human formation categories respecting today's seminarians that must be taken into consideration by formators.

Coincidental with the rise of digital technology and social media has been a major trend in parenting in the United States and the West, which began to take hold in the 1980's and 1990's, and its impact on the human development of young people. It is what Jonathan Haidt refers to as the rise of "fearful parenting", which he says has led to the disappearance of "play-based childhood" and the appearance of "phone-based childhood". According to Haight, children today experience reality through their smartphones and other digital technologies, rather than through experiential interactions with other human beings. The impact of these trends on young people, including those entering seminary, cannot be underestimated and has transformed young peoples' perception and experience of reality in ways that must be understood by anyone interested in human development and maturity. They have caused the young people of today to perceive reality and socialize in completely different ways than in the past. Haidt concludes that the effects of these trends are largely negative with respect to maturation and growth toward becoming self-possessed, confident adults capable of interacting in mature, responsible, and competent ways in navigating the challenges of life, and positive, productive socialization for participation in the communities one belongs to.

Haight discusses "antifragility", a term coined by the social psychologist Nassim Taleb, positing that children are by nature "antifragile". That is, in a healthy, functioning society, children learn from play and other experiences how to navigate the risks inherent in life, and how to recover from mistakes and even injuries when the risks they take in play and everyday life lead to getting hurt, physically or emotionally. He proposes that this is a necessary process for navigating life successfully and having a healthy and satisfying experience of life. Starting in the 1980's, parents and public school authorities increasingly attempted to eliminate risk, getting hurt, and negative experiences from the lives of children, protecting them as much as possible, rather than allowing them to experience the negative and hurtful experiences of life that require resilience in order to function capably and satisfactorily. This led to a phenomenon he refers to as "safetyism", the exact opposite of what children actually need in order to grow and develop into mature, self-confident, competent, adults. If children seldom or never experience the negative consequences they need to navigate and recover from in order to be able to get on with life successfully, their capacity to navigate situations and recover from negative experiences in general is diminished. If they are always protected from negative experiences and negative emotions, they

---

[18] John Byron Kuhner, "Jane Austen Against the Smartphone", *First Things,* January 28, 2025.

come to expect that they will always be protected, and they lose the capacity to navigate and recover. They also become risk-avoidant. Children need to take risks in order to develop self-confidence and the social and other skills necessary to live successful and satisfying lives. If they are preoccupied with avoiding risks, and are afraid of ever experiencing negative consequences, they become extremely anxious—all the time. These psychological dynamics are exacerbated by the social and psychological dynamics of social media: Hence Haidt's "anxious generation".

Children experience negative consequences to varying degrees, of course, but the data is clear that this new psychology of adolescence has become, to a very large extent, normative for the current generation, which includes those entering seminary. Thus, seminary formators concerned with human formation will need to be aware of the social and psychological context seminary candidates are coming from today, will need to assess the appearance of these traits in seminarians, and strategize how to compensate for and remediate the negative consequences in their seminarians if they are going to be able to form priesthood candidates who are not handicapped by these dominant characteristics in young people who have grown up in and been formed by a culture that is marked by "safetyism", overly protective home and school environments, and a "phone-based" rather than "play-based" childhood. The author can attest to having observed all of these characteristics in seminarians over the past twenty-five years,

recognizes the need to take them very seriously and strategize how to overcome them by developing human formation strategies that will be capable of remediating the deficits they result in to form seminarians who are self-possessed, self-confident, secure, capable of taking necessary risks and dealing with the consequences, and who become mature, capable adults capable of manifesting the kind of virtues and character called for by the Church in priestly formation and necessary for assuming the leadership positions priests and pastors are asked to fulfill, and as reflected in the best traditions of human formation and priestly decorum over the long history of priestly formation and priestly behavioral expectations.

Jonathan Haidt's analysis and recommendations provide a rich source of valuable data and psychological and sociological analysis for those involved in seminary formation to understand the candidates entering seminary today. He describes the enormous impact that social media has had on young people born after 1980 that cannot be ignored by anyone who wishes to help those approaching adulthood and adult responsibilities achieve the kind of maturity and personal and social skills they need to navigate life and responsible careers successfully, much less to flourish humanly and individually, and to acquire the capacity to truly be of service in caring professions with significant responsibilities towards others and the communities they serve in. Also to develop the kind of character, personal characteristics, and skills necessary to be effective leaders of those communities, in the case of Catholic priests communities of the Christian faithful, and of complicated institutions that involve difficult leadership challenges. The kind of impacts Haidt identifies have affected in a particular and often in deleterious ways young peoples' self-image, sense of identity, and sense of worth. His analysis is extremely helpful for understanding the psychology of young people today, their suffering, and what needs to be addressed and remedied to assist them in achieving a healthier outlook on themselves and on life in general. Doing so will be necessary to enable them to be fully functioning, healthy, and reasonably satisfied individuals with a positive outlook on life. Those involved in seminary formation are encountering the same psychological characteristics Haidt has identified in young people in general today in seminarians, and the same need to be able to identify the source of these dynamics, address their negative impacts, and bring about healing and liberation from them. The goal is to free seminarians so they can experience the necessary personal and spiritual freedom required for the honest discernment of a priestly vocation, to empower them to be able to make the kind of commitment necessary to pursue that vocation successfully, and in a way that will lead to both a productive and satisfying lives as a Catholic priest.

## Conclusion

The following resources constitute a select bibliography of resources for seminary formators developing and administering human formation programs for their seminaries that will provide them with a broad-based and detailed grasp of the various elements involved in striving towards the kind of human formation called for by Pope St. John Paul II in *PDV* and reflected in the 2016 *Ratio fundamentalis insitutionis sacerdotalis* and *PPF6* of the United States Conference of Catholic Bishops:

St. Ambrose of Milan, *De Officiis*, Edited with an Introduction, Translation, and Commentary by Ivor J. Davidson, Oxford University Press, The Oxford Early Christian Studies Series, (Oxford, 2001).

St. Alphonsus Ligouri, *Dignity and Duties of the Priest; or Selva*, ed. Eugene Grimm, Benzinger Brothers (New York, Cincinnati, Chicago, 1889).

*The Catholic Priest in the United States: Historical Investigations*, ed., John Tracy Ellis, Saint John's University Press (Collegeville, MN, 1971).

Eugene C. Kennedy, M.M., Ph.D. and Victor J. Heckler, Ph.D., *The Catholic Priest in the United States: Psychological Investigations*, Washington, D.C. (United States Catholic Conference, 1972).

The National Opinion Research Center, *The Catholic Priest in the United States: Socio-*

*logical Investigations*, United States Catholic Conference (Washington, D.C., 1972).

Stephen J. Rossetti. *Why Priests are Happy: A Study of Psychological and Spiritual Health of Priests.* Notre Dame, Indiana (Ave Maria Press, 2011).

J. B. Hogan, S.S., D.D., *Clerical Studies*, Marlier & company, Ltd. (Boston 1898).

Jonathan Haidt, *The Anxious Generation*, Penguin Press (New York, NY, 2024).

Jean Piaget:

1. Howard Gardner, *The Quest for Mind: Piaget, Levi-Strauss and the Structuralist Movement*, (University of Chicago Press, (1981).
2. Harry *Beilin, "Piaget's Enduring Contribution to Developmental Psychology". Developmental Psychology. 28 (2): 191–204.*
3. *Serhat Kurt, "Jean Piaget: Biography, Theory and Cognitive Development", Education Library, (17 November 2022).*
4. Kendra *Cherry, "Piaget's 4 Stages of Cognitive Development Explained", https:// www.verywellmind.com, (1 May 2024).*
5. John W. Santrock, *Children*, New York, NY (McGraw-Hill,1998).

Abraham Maslow:

1. *A. H. Maslow, "A theory of human motivation", Psychological Review. 50 (4): 370-396, Cite SeerX 10.1.1.334. 7586, 10.1037/h0054346, doi:10.1037/ h00g4346, S2CID 53326433.*
3. W. B. Frick, "Interview with Dr. Abraham Maslow", in *Humanistic psychology: Conversations with Abraham Maslow, Gardner Murphy, Carl Rogers* (pp. 19–50). Bristol, IN: Wyndham Hall Press. (1989, original work published 1971).
2. A. H. *Maslow, "A Theory of Metamotivation: The Biological Rooting of the Value-Life". Journal of Humanistic Psychology. 7 (2): 93–126,* (1967), *doi:10.1177/002216786700700201. S2 CID 145703009.*
3. N. R. Carlson, et al., *Psychology: The Science of Behaviour.* 4th Canadian ed. Toronto, ON (Pearson Education Canada, 2007).
4. Kathleen Stassen Berger, *The Developing Person through the Life Span*, (Worth Publishers; Eleventh edition, December 23, 2019).
5. A. H. Maslow, "A Theory of Human Motivation", in *Psychological Review*, 50 (4), 430-437, (Washington, DC: American Psychological Association, 1943).

6.  David M. Brookman, "Maslow's Hierarchy and Student Retention", *NACADA Journal*, v.9 n.1 pp. 69–74, Spring 1989.

7.  R. Villa, J. Thousand, W. Stainback, S. Stainback, "Restructuring for Caring & Effective Education", Baltimore, (Paul Brookes, 1992)

8.  Michael R. Hagerty, "Testing Maslow's Hierarchy of Needs: National Quality-of-Life Across Time", Social Indicators Research 46(xx), 1999, 250.

9.  *Aron, Adrianne, "Maslow's Other Child", Journal of Humanistic Psychology, 17 (2): 13.*

10. Thierry *Pauchan, Collette A. Dumas,* "Abraham Maslow and Heinz Kohut: *A Comparison", Journal of Humanistic Psychology.* **31** *(2):* 58. doi:10. 1177/0022167891312005. S2CID 145 440463.

11. D. G. *Myers, Social psychology (11th ed., New York (McGraw-Hill, 1999), pp. 11–12.*

12. Richard H. *Lowry, The Journals of A.H. Maslow Vol. 1., Monterey, CA (Brooks/Cole Publishing Co., 1979), p. 232.*

13. *C. George Boeree,* "Abraham Maslow," archived *from the original on October 24, 2009.*

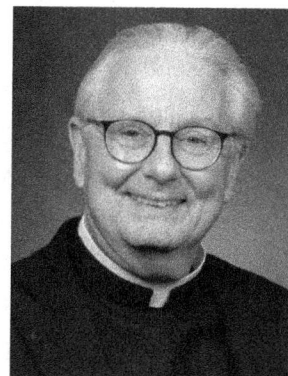

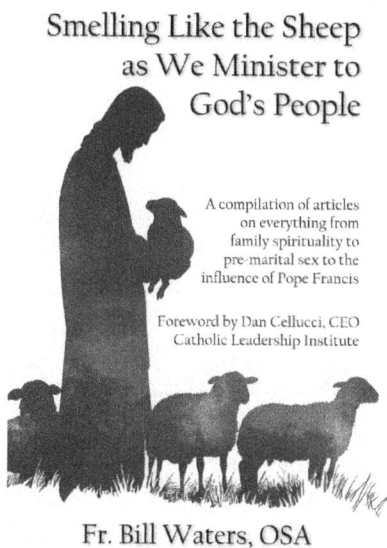

# The Diocesan Priest and Seminary Formation

## Most Reverend Fredrik Hansen, J.C.L., J.C.D., D.D.

### Introduction

As part of its broader introduction to seminary formation, the current *Program of Priestly Formation*[1] offers an important theological exposition on the ministerial priesthood in sections 23-36. Among the key insights found therein is what the document refers to as "ecclesiological expression" of priestly identity: "The priest's specific configuration to Christ brings about this special relationship to his Body, the Church. Within the Body, he represents Christ, Head and Shepherd, Servant and Spouse, as a co-worker with the bishop. The nature and mission of the ministerial priesthood can only be fully understood within the mystery of the Church, as a service to the glory of God and to the brothers and sisters in their baptismal priesthood" (*PPF6* 28). The document goes on to highlight three specific features that are of crucial importance for the diocesan priest: his ministry in the particular church, his communion with his bishop, and his fraternal collaboration with his brother priests. This article seeks to elaborate on these realities and how they are to be expressed in diocesan seminary formation.

> "This article seeks to elaborate on three specific features that are of crucial importance for the diocesan priest: his ministry in the particular church, his communion with his bishop, and his fraternal collaboration with his brother priests, and how these are to be expressed in diocesan seminary formation."

### The Diocesan Presbyter

Most seminaries in the United States provide formation for candidates to the diocesan priesthood. Part of that formation must, therefore, be aimed at instilling in the seminarians a truly diocesan spirit, configuring future priests by laying the groundwork for real and lasting bonds to their diocesan bishop, to their particular churches (dioceses)[2] and to their diocesan

---

[1] United States Conference of Catholic Bishops, *Program of Priestly Formation in the United States of America.* 6th ed. (USCCB, 2022). [Henceforth: *PPF6*.]

[2] Unless otherwise evident from context, the article uses "particular church" and "diocese" interchangeable, in accordance with the understanding that dioceses are the archetype of a particular church: "Particular churches, in which and from which the one and only Catholic Church exists, are first of all dioceses." Canon Law Society of America, *Code of Canon Law. Latin-English Edition. New English Translation.* 4th printing (CLSA, 2023), can. 368.

presbyterate. This is, in fact, expressly called for in the *Ratio fundamentalis*: "With a view to service in a particular Church, seminarians are called to acquire the spirituality of a diocesan priest, which is characterized by selfless dedication to the ecclesiastical circumscription to which they belong, or to the one in which they will in fact exercise the ministry, for the diocesan priest is the shepherd and servant of all in a specific context."[3]

A 'diocesan priest' may be defined as a presbyter[4] incardinated into a particular church or an ecclesial structure equivalent to a particular church. The starting point for this definition is the diocesan priest's relationship to his diocese. Its theological and ecclesiological impact is, however, far broader as the diocesan bishop and the diocesan presbyterate are inherent to the diocese as a particular church. The *Code of Canon Law* articulates this in its succinct definition of a diocese: "a portion of the people of God which is entrusted to a bishop for him to shepherd with the cooperation of the presbyterium" (can. 369), a text drawn from the conciliar degree *Christus Dominus*.[5]

It seems opportune to comment briefly on use of the term 'secular priest,' which in recent years has largely fallen out of use. This has occurred for two reasons. First, because the term 'secular priest' defines the diocesan priests in comparison to religious or regular priests, lending itself to a "negative" understanding of the diocesan priest: he is a priest who is *not* religious or regular. Second, because the term 'secular' suggests that the diocesan priest—again unlike religious or regular priests—is in some fashion "of the world." By way of example of the use of 'secular priest' and, at the same time, confirmation of its inadequacies, one reference book states: "Secular clergy are not members of a religious institute or society of apostolic life, so they are not considered 'regular,' i.e., obliged to follow a rule (Lat., *regula*) of religious life. Because they do not withdraw from the world (Lat., *saeculum*) in the same way religious vow to do, they are

> "A 'diocesan priest' may be defined as a presbyter incardinated into a particular church or an ecclesial structure equivalent to a particular church. The starting point for this definition is the diocesan priest's relationship to his diocese."

---

[3] Congregation for Clergy, *The Gift of the Priestly Vocation. Ratio Fundamentalis Institutionis Sacerdotalis* (Libreria Editrice Vaticana, 2016), 71. [Henceforth: *Ratio*.]

[4] Following general practice, the article uses the terms 'presbyter' and 'priest' interchangeably. The stricter canonical approach taken by the *Code of Canon Law* is to use the term 'priest' to describe both a presbyter and a bishop—describing the two holy orders that "receive the mission and capacity to act in the person of Christ the Head" (can. 1009 §3).

[5] Second Vatican Council, Decree *Christus Dominus*. In *Decrees of the Ecumenical Councils*, ed. Norman Tanner, vol 2. (Georgetown University Press, 1990). [Hereafter: *CD*.] The conciliar degree defined a diocese as a "section of the people of God whose pastoral care is entrusted to a bishop in cooperation with his priests" (*CD* 8). It should be noted that the Latin original for both "portion" in the Code and "section" in *CD* is the same: "portio."

called 'secular.'"[6] The term 'diocesan,' on the other hand, is both positive in nature and spiritually more fruitful because of its innate connection with the diocese—marking and identifying the priest by that very bond to his diocese, the diocesan bishop, and diocesan presbyterate.

It must further be recalled that priestly ordination, the promises a diocesan priest makes at ordination, and his incardination in the diocese result in a very specific consecration and way of life. Ordination itself confers "the dignity of priesthood" and the ordination prayer spoken by the bishop calls on God to "renew deep within [those ordained] the Spirit of holiness."[7] The ordination promises—while clearly not a rule of religious life—lay upon each diocesan priest the yoke of Christ and serve as an entryway to the spirituality of the diocesan priest as in them are captured his ministerial and interior life. Among the promises—and intimately connected to a diocesan priest's service in the diocese—is the one concerning unity with Christ and consecration to service, formulated in the following question the bishop asks the ordinand: "Do you resolve to be united more closely every day to Christ the High Priest, who offered himself for us to the Father as a pure sacrifice, and with him to consecrate yourself to God for the salvation of all?" The priest recalls this conformity to Our Lord in the vesting prayer of the chasuble: "*Domine, qui dixisti: Jugum meum suave est et onus meum leve: fac, ut*

*istud portare sic valeam, quod consequar tuam gratiam.*" A diocesan priests incardination in a diocese provides what the *Ratio fundamentalis* refers to as the "specific context"—being not only the place of his ministry, but also the particular portion of the People of God for which he is called to make a "selfless dedication to the ecclesiastical circumscription" (*Ratio* 71), abandoning himself and the world in the Holy Spirit and consecrating himself with Christ to the Father.

In light of the above, it is clear that seminary formation of diocesan candidates must include prayer about, profound study of, and detailed instruction in the rite of ordination, the meaning and demands of the priestly promises, and the role of a diocesan priest's service to his diocese. A coherent and distinct understanding of diocesan priestly spirituality should also be advanced among the seminarians —and one that they not only understand, but one that they assume and live out, first

> **"Seminary formation of diocesan candidates must include prayer about, profound study of, and detailed instruction in the rite of ordination, the meaning and demands of the priestly promises, and the role of a diocesan priest's service to his diocese."**

[6] *The HarperCollins Encyclopedia of Catholicism*, ed. Richard P. McBrien (HarperCollins, 1995), 324.

[7] *The Roman Pontifical Renewed by Decree of the Most Holy Second Ecumenical Council of the Vatican, Promulgated by Authority of Pope Paul VI and Revised at the Direction of Pope John Paul II, Ordination of a Bishop, of Priests, and of Deacons, English Translation According to the Second Typical Edition for Use in the Dioceses of the United States of America* (USCCB, 2021) 131.

in seminary, and then in priestly life and ministry.

## Belonging to and Ministering in a Diocese

The Second Vatican Council's decree on the ministry of bishops speaks of diocesan priests as those presbyters who are "incardinated or attached to a particular church, for they have fully dedicated themselves in the service of caring for a single portion of the Lord's flock" (*CD* 28). The bond with the diocese is expressed, in other words, through incardination and dedication to ministry in and for a particular church.

The "selfless dedication" expresses itself and begins to take shape long before diaconal ordination and incardination. A young man will as part of his initial discernment identify the diocese for which he feels called to undertake vocational discernment and ministerial formation. While that will in most circumstances be the one in which his familial home is located, it may also be the diocese in which he has studied or worked more recently, the diocese from which his family originally hails or due to some other bond. In all these reasons is found a felt rootedness in a diocese, a familiarity with its reality and pastoral life, and a desire to contribute to that as a sacred minister. In most cases, the future diocesan priest will have been actively engaged in parish or pastoral life, thereby laying the groundwork for a later priestly ministry and presbyteral brotherhood. With this as background, the young man who senses a call to priesthood identifies a diocese "for whose service" (can. 266 §1) he will be advanced towards ordination through seminary formation upon acceptance by the diocesan bishop.[8] This becomes the diocese which he is to come to know, the people he is to serve, the presbyterate he will eventually join and the diocesan bishop to which he will promise obedience.

As the conciliar exposition from *Christus Dominus* above affirms, through a priest's service a specific bond between him and the "portion of the People of God" that constitute the diocese is established. That bond is not to the geographic circumscription of the diocese, but to the faithful—the "portion." As expressed in *Lumen Gentium*,[9] it is for the faithful (and not for himself) that a presbyter is "consecrated as true priests of the new testament, to preach the gospel and nourish the faithful and celebrate divine worship. … it is above all in the eucharistic worship or synaxis that they exercise their sacred function … acting in the person of Christ" (*LG* 28). The very existence of the priesthood is ministerial (for service) and relational (for others): "The reason for the existence of the priesthood is to be found and discovered in the mystery of the Church, the Mystical Body of Christ and the People of God journeying through history, which has been established as the universal sacrament of salva-

---

[8] The *Program for Priestly Formation* notes that "it is the responsibility of the diocesan bishop … to decide whether to admit applicants into priestly formation, in accordance with the criteria which have been properly established" (*PPF6*, 56).

[9] Second Vatican Council, Dogmatic constitution *Lumen Gentium*. In *Decrees of the Ecumenical Councils*, ed. Norman Tanner, vol 2. (Georgetown University Press, 1990). [Henceforth: *LG*.]

tion."[10] For the diocesan priest, his ministry and relationality becomes concrete in his diocese, is sharpened by his years of familiarity with the faithful of the diocese and their circumstances, and allows him to see—albeit in small ways or only over a lifetime of ministry—the fruits of his labors among his own people.

A seminarian's time spent in pastoral assignments, in retreats or on breaks in his home diocese are, as a result of the above, valuable *loci* of formation for diocesan priesthood. This includes also more structured presentation on and learning experiences in his diocese, prolonged ministry in various parishes (of different sizes, geographical location, socio-economic reality etc.) during his time of seminary formation, and—as per the sections below—time spent with both bishop and presbyterate.

Incardination is the legal institute by which the diocesan priest's specific belonging to a particular Church is expressed canonically. While incardination comes about at diaconal ordination (can. 266 §1), this bond between the cleric and his diocese endures and continues to have effect also after presbyteral ordination. Canonical legislation demands that every cleric or sacred minister in the Church must be incardinated into an ecclesiastical structure.[11] This is to rule out any kind of "acephalous or wandering clergy" (can. 265), the existence of which has caused the Church, the priesthood and the faithful great problems and indeed much scandal over the centuries.[12] Only the legal act of excardination—not the mere moving to another diocese (for example to study or minister)—releases a cleric from his incardination in his particular church and incardinates him into another particular church (can. 267).

"A seminarian's time spent in pastoral assignments, in retreats or for rest in his home diocese are valuable loci of formation for diocesan priesthood."

Incardination is, however, not only a juridic reality: "Incardination, or incorporation as a sacred minister to a particular church or comparative entity is, therefore, a juridic relationship which joins a cleric to the bishop and which also unites him to a presbyterate and to other members of the faithful."[13] This relationship is ecclesiological—bringing about and continuing to affirm the ministerial and spiritual bonds that exist between a sacred minister and the particular church, the diocesan bishop, and

---

[10] Congregation for Clergy, Instruction *Priest, Pastor and Leader of the Parish Community* (Libreria Editrice Vaticana, 2002), 5. [Henceforth: *Instruction.*]

[11] Canon 265 identifies the various ecclesial institution into which a cleric may be incardination: "in a particular church or personal prelature, or in an institute of consecrated life or society endowed with this faculty, or also in a public clerical association that has obtained this faculty from the Apostolic See."

[12] Francis J. Schneider, "Chapter II. The Enrollment, or Incardination, of Clerics," in *New Commentary on the Code of Canon Law*, ed. John P. Beal (Paulist Press, 2000) 330, sub can. 265.

[13] "Chapter II. The Enrollment or Incardination of Clerics," in *Exegetical Commentary on the Code of Canon Law*, ed. Ernest Caparros (Wilson & Lafleur/Midwest Theological Forum, 2004) 2/1:302, sub can. 265.

the presbyterate.[14] Where the priest is incardinated identifies his ecclesial "home," the *locus* of his priestly ministry, and his priestly father (the bishop) and priestly brothers (the presbyterate).[15]

Incardination must be adequately explained in seminary formation, both from a canonical and an ecclesiological perspective. While clearly a juridic institute, incardination speaks volumes about a priest's belonging to his diocese and his identity as a diocesan priest. Such an approach—rooted in both canon law and ecclesiology—facilitates further an understanding of the gravity of diaconal ordination, which enrolls the diocesan seminarian among the sacred ministers of the Church, "who in law are also called clerics" (can. 207 §1), and incardinates him into his diocese.

## "Co-Worker" of the Diocesan Bishop

The two presbyteral decrees of the Second Vatican Council—*Presbyterorum ordinis*[16] on the ministry of priests and *Optatam totius*[17] on the formation of priests—build on the theological teaching of the Council found in the dogmatic constitution *Lumen Gentium*. These three and all post-conciliar magisterial documents on the priesthood underscore the priest's essential bond to the bishop—the dependence of the presbyteral order on the episcopal order. *Lumen Gentium* succinctly states the following: "Priests, although they do not possess the highest degree of the priesthood, and although they are dependent on the bishops in the exercise of their power, nevertheless they are united with the bishops in sacerdotal dignity" (*LG* 28).

It is, unsurprising therefore, that "seminaries should inculcate in each seminarian a capacity to live in communion with his diocesan bishop" (*PPF6*, 219). Or the point made more directly: "He learns that offering his life in service to the Church involves understanding and following the will of Christ in the person of his diocesan bishop" (*PPF6*, 378). This relationship between the priest and his bishop begins even before a candidate undertakes formal seminary studies. It falls to the diocesan bishop to accept men

> "Where the priest is incardinated identifies his ecclesial "home," the locus of his priestly ministry, and his priestly father (the bishop) and priestly brothers (the presbyterate)."

---

[14] Giangiacomo Sarzi Sartori, "L'incardinazione in una Chiesa particolare," *Quaderni di diritto ecclesiale* 15 (2002) 124.

[15] Sarzi Sartori points to the ministerial and ecclesial importance of incardination at Vatican II as leading to a more expanded understanding, one that did, however, not remove or minimize the juridic and canonical role of incardination: "Il Vaticano II segna una svolta fondamentale favorendo un concetto di incardinazione che, senza pregiudicarne gli scopi disciplinari, vuole restituire all'istituto il suo originario significato pastorale ed esplicitarne la valenza in ordine al servizio ministeriale ed ecclesiale. Sartori, "L'incardinazione," 133.

[16] Second Vatican Council, Decree *Presbyterorum ordinis*. In *Decrees of the Ecumenical Councils*, ed. Norman Tanner, vol 2. (Georgetown University Press, 1990). [Henceforth: *PO*.]

[17] Second Vatican Council, Decree *Optatam totius*. In *Decrees of the Ecumenical Councils*, ed. Norman Tanner, vol 2. (Georgetown University Press, 1990). [Henceforth: *OT*.]

into formation, a process that tends to include some individual engagement between the two. It is also to be presumed that a would-be-seminarian would have some knowledge of his bishop even before meeting him as part of the admissions process. The seminary should—through its formation program and in close collaboration with the diocesan vocations director—facilitate and encourage seminarians to attend episcopal liturgies and meet regularly with their diocesan bishop.

The relationship between a priest and his bishop may be understood under two headings: one theological and one canonical-pastoral. In terms of theology, priests "in union with bishops, so share in one and the same priesthood and ministry of Christ that the very unity of their consecration and mission requires their hierarchical communion with the order of bishops" (*PO* 7). The presbyteral and episcopal order are bound together as 'holy orders,' as grades of the sacrament of ordination. The origin of that unity is above all Christ, who is the origin of all priesthood in the Church (*PO* 1). With its solemn affirmation that "the fullness of the sacrament of order is conferred by episcopal consecration" (*LG* 21), the Council identified the episcopate as the primary holy order and, therefore, the two others—presbyterate and diaconate—as stemming from and being of assistance to the episcopate. The most obvious expression of this is that the rite of incorporating a man into the presbyteral or diaconal order is celebrated by a bishop (can. 1012)—it is the episcopal order that confers the two others.

As for the canonical-pastoral bond between priest and bishop, the starting point is the priest's promise of obedience. Like the other ordination promises, that of obedience takes the form of the bishop's question to the ordinand: "Do you promise respect and obedience to me and my successors?" The Council sees this promise as another expression of the presbyteral order's share in the episcopal order's apostolic ministry, the unity of the sacrament of orders, and the theological pre-eminence of the episcopal order: "This priestly obedience, imbued with a spirit of cooperation is based on the very sharing in the episcopal ministry which is conferred on priests both through the Sacrament of Orders and the canonical mission" (*PO* 7). Priests' share in the bishop's ministry means that they are "[a]ssociated with their bishop in a spirit of trust and generosity, they make him present in a certain sense in the individual local congregations, and take upon themselves, as far as they are able, his duties and the burden of his care, and discharge them with a daily interest" (*LG* 28). While the participation of priests in the one priesthood of Christ and co-operation with the episcopal order is hierarchical, it remains "specifically sacramental in nature and hence cannot be interpreted in merely 'organisational' terms."[18] A priest is, in other words, not an

---

[18] Congregation for Clergy, *Directory on the Life and Ministry of Priests*. Revised ed. (Libreria Editrice Vaticana, 2013) 6. [Henceforth: *Directory*.]

inferior functionary of the diocesan bishop—he is the bishop's sacramental co-worker.

In the decree *Christus Dominus*, the Council notes the "various relationships between the bishop and his diocesan priests should be held together most of all by the bonds of supernatural charity" (*CD* 28). The goal of this is to ensure that the communion between priests and bishop "make their pastoral work more fruitful" (*CD* 28). In the background stands once more the Lord as the origin of sacred ministry and His example and model of all such ministry as the Good Shepherd. Much like the ministry and rootedness in the particular church impacts the spirituality of the diocesan priest, so does the bond with the diocesan bishop. Pope Francis articulated—with his characteristic poignancy—this principle as follows: a diocesan priest "cannot be separated from the Bishop" and that there "is no spirituality of the diocesan priest without these two relationships: with the Bishop and with the presbytery."[19]

Seminary formation must give particular attention to the unity and bonds between the episcopal and presbyteral order and between a diocesan priest and his diocesan bishop. Rightly so, the *Program of Priestly Formation* demands that a "separate course on Holy Orders, with a thorough study of the nature and mission of the ministerial priesthood including a history and theology of celibacy, is required" (*PPF6*, 328). An incorrect theology of priesthood could very easily lead to a deeply flawed understanding of both the presbyter and the bishop, and the mutual dependence that exist between these two sacerdotal degrees of the sacrament of holy orders. This would most adversely impact both the individual seminarian and certainly have consequences for his pastoral ministry in the diocese post-ordination.

> "A priest is not an inferior functionary of the diocesan bishop—he is the bishop's sacramental co-worker."

The more specifically pastoral relationship between priest and bishop comes to the fore in the priest working with, on behalf of, and exercising a ministry in complete accord with his bishop. He in turn is expected to faithfully implement the pastoral ministry of the Church, articulated under the *tria munera Christi* in *Lumen Gentium* 25-27 and further specified in canons 383-398 and expounded upon greatly in the directory *Apostolores successores*.[20] While the pastor is entrusted with guiding his parish community and leading its pastoral life, and other priestly offices also have scope for pastoral ingenuity and direction from the priest, the broader pastoral vision of the bishop is to be the starting point. The same applies to the unity with the diocesan bishop, which allows the priestly ministry

---

[19] Pope Francis, "Comments during the Meeting with the Priests of the Diocese of Caserta," in *Disciples Together on the Road. Words of Pope Francis for Priests* (Libreria Editrice Vaticana, 2016) 50.

[20] Congregation for Bishops, Directory *Apostolorum successores* (Libreria Editrice Vaticana, 2004). Chapters IV to VIII of the directory concern, in one way or another, the governing responsibility of the diocesan bishop in the particular church entrusted to his care. In chapter IV, sections 75 to 83 are dedicated to the oversight a diocesan bishop is to exercise over the presbyterium.

to contribute to the broader communion of the diocese. Speaking of the role of the pastor in particular, the Congregation for Clergy noted that he is "obliged to collaborate with his Bishop and with the other priests of the diocese so as to ensure that the faithful who participate in the parochial community become aware that they are also members of the diocese" (*Instruction* 22).

> "Advancing an active understanding of the inseparability of the priest from the episcopal office, not only in pastoral ministry, but also in presbyteral life and spirituality is key."

Further to the canonical and theological bonds, the Church understands there to a strong paternal and fraternal bond between a bishop and his priests: "on account of this communion in the same priesthood and ministry, bishops should regard priests as their brothers and friends" (*PO* 7). These fraternal and paternal bonds lay a specific charge on the bishop, who is to "attend to presbyters and listen to them as assistants and counselor. He is to protect their rights and take care that they correctly fulfill the obligations proper to their state ..." (can. 384). Pope John Paul II expanded on this canonical norm by noting that the diocesan bishop "will always strive to relate to his priests as a father and brother who loves them, listens to them, welcomes them, corrects them, supports them, seeks their cooperation and, as much as possible, is

concerned for their human, spiritual, ministerial and financial well-being."[21] Priests carry out a necessary and important service in the diocese, are familiar with its realities and challenges, and provide the bishop with fraternal and filial support and advise. This should be welcomed by the bishop, recognizing both his own unity with the presbyterate and the collaborative nature of the priest-bishop relationship. In fact, the Council states that bishops "should gladly listen to their priests, indeed consult them and engage in dialogue with them in those matters which concern the necessities of pastoral work and welfare of the diocese" (*PO* 7). Pope Paul VI advanced this idea by noting that a bishop's paternal oversight of his priests will transform their juridic obedience into a sense of pastoral charity: "Before being the superiors and judges of your priests, be their teachers, fathers, friends, their good and kind brothers ... This will not weaken the relationship of juridical obedience; rather it will transform it into pastoral love so that they will obey more willingly, sincerely and securely."[22]

Promoting an active understanding of the inseparability of the priest from the episcopal office, not only in pastoral ministry, but also in presbyteral life and spirituality is key. The same applies to promoting the regular participation in the life of the seminary of the diocesan bishop of the diocese in which the seminary is located, governing diocesan bishop(s), and sending diocesan bishops. Instructing seminarians on the importance of a proper disposition as concern

[21] Pope John Paul II, Post-synodal Apostolic Exhortation *Pastores gregis* (Libreria Editrice Vaticana, 2003), 47.

[22] Pope Paul VI, Encyclical Letter *Sacerdotalis Cælibatus* (Our Sunday Visitor, 1967), 93.

collaborative ministry with the diocesan bishop is vital, therefore, to a truly diocesan formation. This covers both an open and docile attitude in general to the bishop and a desire to be of assistance to the bishop. At times, this will call for the giving of advice and the expression of concern. At other times, it will consist of the assumption of duties that the priest may be reluctant to assume, but that in consultation with the bishop and for the good of the diocese he assumes, nonetheless. The promise of obedience that the priest makes to his bishop (and successors) is of vital importance. Care should be taken to assist seminarians in avoiding a simplistic and servile blind obedience on the one hand, as well as an individualistic, negative and confrontational approach to the bishop and his governance and leadership on the other.

## Diocesan Presbyter and His Brother Presbyters

In its presentation on the presbyteral order, *Presbyterorum ordinis* notes that priests, "by virtue of their ordination to the priesthood are united among themselves in an intimate sacramental brotherhood" (*PO* 8). Ordination—to the diaconate, presbyterate, or the episcopate—is the being made part of an 'ordo,' being assumed into a body of individuals who are joined one to another.[23] Presbyteral ordination includes among its many liturgical signs and rites two specific expressions of the ordinand being taken up into the

priestly order: the imposition of hands and the fraternal sign of peace. On the latter, the Congregation for Clergy affirmed that the "rite of the imposition of the hands during the priestly ordination by the bishop and all the priests present harbors special significance insofar as it indicates both equality of participation in the ministry and the fact that the priest cannot act by himself, but always within the presbyterate, becoming a brother of all those who constitute it" (*Directory* 34).

This "intimate brotherhood" exists among all priests, regardless of their "home" (in a particular church or an institute of consecrated life) or their specific ministry (parochial, curial, monastic, etc.). The ultimate source of this unity among all priests is Christ, and its hierarchical source is the bishop: all priests, "in union with bishops, so share in one and the same priesthood and ministry of Christ that the very unity of their consecration and mission requires their hierarchical communion with the order of bishops" (*PO* 7). While not impacting the universal presbyteral unity, a further, more specific, and often far-more specific bond exists among those priests who minister within the same particular church, and even more so among priests that are also bound to that diocese: the incardinated diocesan presbyterate.

What the teaching of the Church makes plain is that priestly "fraternity and membership in a presbyterate are therefore elements characterizing the priest" (*Directory* 34). The presbyterate in a diocese may, therefore, be defined as being for

---

[23] *Catechism of the Catholic Church*, 2nd ed. (United States Conference of Catholic Bishops, 2019) 1537.

the diocesan presbyter "the company of the priests of his own diocese assembled around their bishop, their spiritual father and ruler, the center and the principle of unity in their sacerdotal community."[24] Noticeable once more is the centrality of the diocesan bishop for his priests and the bonds that unite the priests among themselves and to their bishop.[25]

It will be vital for seminary formation to underscore and transmit to diocesan seminarians the point made by Pope John Paul II in *Pastores dabo vobis*: the "ordained ministry has a radical 'communitarian form' and can only be carried out as a 'collective work'."[26] Priestly ministry is never a solitary or self-reliant ministry. The diocesan priest is—in both his priestly identify and his priestly ministry—never alone. He is bound to his bishop and to his brother priests. While the practical reality of many diocesan priests is ministry as pastor in a parish (or several) with no other priests on staff or in residence, the "collective work" of priestly ministry remains. This as, "[i]n individual dioceses, priests

> **"The seminary must instruct the seminarians on the theological, ecclesiological and canonical unity of the diocesan presbyterate."**

form one priesthood under their own bishop" (*PO* 8).

Therefore, the seminary—as a formational community—"leads the seminarian, through ordination, to become part of the 'family' of the presbyterate, at the service of a particular community" (*Ratio* 3). The seminary must, therefore, instruct the seminarians on the theological, ecclesiological and canonical unity of the diocesan presbyterate. This is advance by the modelling on the part of priest faculty of solid presbyteral fraternity, and the promotion among seminarians—as diocesan groups and as a seminary community—a fraternal spirit and sound practical expressions of that spirit. The seminary as a whole, composed of both seminarians and formators, should advance a collegial approach to presbyteral ministry and life, recognizing that a priest is not a lone minister or independent pastoral worker, but rather one assumed into and active within a specific presbyterate of the diocesan bishop and diocesan presbyters. It will, furthermore, be important to encourage that the seminarians meet and engage with the presbyterate of their diocese—their future brothers in the diocesan priesthood.

---

[24] Joseph C. Fenton, *The Diocesan Priest in the Church of Christ* (Cluny Media, 2018) 17.

[25] The Congregation for Clergy pointed out that belonging to a particular presbyterate—a diocesan priest belonging to his diocesan presbyterate—comes about, not by incardination, but "in the context of a "Episcopal mission" (*Directory* 34). This places the diocesan bishop, the diocese, and the priestly promise of obedience to his bishop and his collaboration with the episcopal order of his bishop as the

factors that bring about that belonging, in addition to the unity among priests based in Christ (origin of priesthood), in the Church (where every priesthood finds its expression and purpose), and the service to the People of God (for which the ministerial priesthood was established).

[26] Pope John Paul II. Post-synodal Apostolic Exhortation *Pastores dabo vobis* (Our Sunday Visitor, 1998) 17. [Henceforth: PDV.]

## Conclusion

Pope John Paul II affirmed the three diocesan bonds in *Pastores dabo vobis* when he observed that the "ministry of priests is above all communion and a responsible and necessary cooperation with the bishop's ministry, in concern … for the individual particular churches, for whose service they form with the bishop a single presbyterate" (*PDV* 17). The Church understands priestly ministry as a crucial means to holiness, the pathway by which a priest unites himself with the life and virtues and holiness of the Good Shepherd.

Vatican II notes that priests "who perform their duties sincerely and indefatigably in the Spirit of Christ arrive at holiness by this very fact" (*PO* 13). The profound connections between the diocesan priest and his bishop, presbyterate and diocese offers a specific context into which that priest finds his life and ministry. Those bonds should also advance in him an ever deeper interior life through the living out of the spirit of Christ's holiness, the truth of Christ's virtues, and the communion of Christ's mysteries.[27]

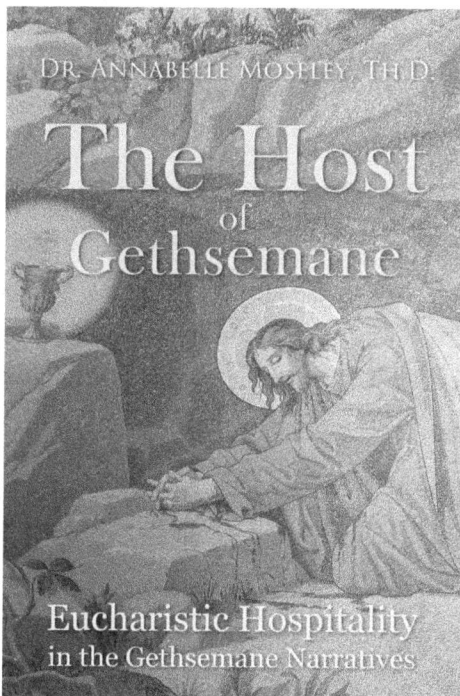

DR. ANNABELLE MOSELEY, TH.D.

**The Host of Gethsemane**

Eucharistic Hospitality
in the Gethsemane Narratives

Most Reverend Fredrik Hansen, J.C.L., J.C.D., D.D.
(fredrik.hansen@katolsk.no)

Bishop Hansen of Oslo, Norway, taught for two years at St. Mary's as Assistant Professor of Pastoral Studies and also served as Dean of Seminarians during that time.

---

*The Host of Gethsemane* is a deeply researched field guide to the profound significance of the Garden of Gethsemane. It is a labor not only of study, but of love—a **defense** of Jesus of Gethsemane in every sense of the word. *The Host of Gethsemane* remedies this abandonment of Our Lord's Agony.

Only $19.95. Available at https://enroutebooksandmedia.com/thehostofgethsemane/

---

[27] From the prayer *O, Jesu, living in Mary* attributed Jean Jacques Olier (1608-1657), founder of the Society of Priests of Saint Sulpice.

# The Intersection of Pastoral Care and Contemporary Leadership in Seminary Formation

## Leelamma Sebastian, M.A., M.S.C.P.

The formation of priests in a Catholic seminary is a comprehensive process encompassing various dimensions – human, intellectual, spiritual, and pastoral. The pastoral dimension is the capstone in which a seminarian implements his theological studies from the classroom in supervised ministerial settings. The *Program of Priestly Formation* 6th edition, one of the official documents that guide seminarian formation, states: "The aim of pastoral formation [is the] formation of a 'true shepherd' who teaches, sanctifies, and governs or leads."[1]

The mission of pastoral formation at St. Mary's Seminary & University is to develop effective pastors who can accompany people in a community on their journey to God. In addition to classroom studies and supervised field assignments, the seminary must integrate insights from modern secular leadership models into programs that form true shepherds of the Catholic Church. In this article, I will explore the essence of pastoral care, the intersection of ministerial and secular leadership, the Sulpician model of pastoral formation, and St. Mary's particular integration of both ministerial and leadership components into pastoral formation in order to prepare seminarians to lead their communities in a ministry of love.

## The Essence of Pastoral Care

Jesus set the standard for pastoral care. "I am the Good Shepherd. A good shepherd lays down his life for the sheep," John 10:11[2] The image of the Good Shepherd echoes in our language about priestly ministry. 1 Pet. 5:2-3 urges presbyters to "Tend the flock of God… [as] examples to the flock." Psalm 23 speaks of a Shepherd who truly shepherds his sheep. Pope Francis encourages priests to "… lead like shepherds and smell like [your] flock. Be shepherds with the odor of the sheep; make it real, as shepherds among your flock, [as] fishers of men."[3] Just as shepherds

---

[1] United States Conference of Catholic Bishops, *Program of Priestly Formation In the United States of America,* 6th edition. (Washington: USCCB, 2022), no. 370, (Hereafter referred to as PPF).

[2] All Scripture quotations come from *The Catholic Study Bible: New American Bible Revised Edition,* 3rd ed. (Oxford: Oxford University Press, 2015).

[3] Francis, "Homily of Pope Francis," Chrism Mass, *Vatican Website,* March 28, 2013, accessed July 30, 2024, https://www.vatican.va/content/francesco/en/homilies/2013/documents/papa-francesco_20130328_messa-crismale.html.

know and love their sheep, priests as leaders must know and love their people.

Jesus is the only one who fulfilled these duties completely, but, *in persona Christi*, priests follow in his footsteps. Pastoral care aims to personify the Good Shepherd's ministry of love. The ministry of presence and listening embodies qualities such as empathy, compassion, and selflessness. The ministry of presence is about "being" rather than "doing." Giving our time and energy to a situation requires freedom from distractions. Pastoral care calls for interior freedom, in order to love the person before us.

Becoming true servants of Christ requires holistic preparation and commitment. After speaking to Pope Francis, Sam Sawyer, S.J., reflects on what he learned from Pope Francis:

It is God who reaches out to us, God who "pastors" first. Pope Francis spoke frequently about a triad that he refers to as God's style of closeness, compassion and tenderness. He means that it is God who pastors first: the Father draws close to our humanity in the gift of the Son, and the Holy Spirit draws us into their love. That is the model—or even better, the mystery—that *pastoralidad* [pastorality] attempts to name. Rather than practical considerations 'limiting' otherwise absolute theological truths, God's own

pastoral closeness to us and our call to embody such compassion ourselves is the central theological truth Pope Francis keeps returning to.[4]

The example of the Good Shepherd is a guiding light for pastoral care and ministry, highlighting the transformative power of love in leadership. Transformation must first occur within the priest, in both heart and actions, before it can touch the hearts of those whom he serves. Our goal in seminary formation is to instill in seminarians the desire to become "whom they contemplate."[5] This grace can be achieved only through prayer, contemplation, and action, which are the foundational sources of pastoral leadership.

> "The example of the Good Shepherd is a guiding light for pastoral care and ministry, highlighting the transformative power of love in leadership."

### Leadership: Secular & Spiritual Insights

The secular understanding of leadership has evolved in the past 100 years. A key early definition of leadership was published in 1927 by B.V. Moore, who wrote that leadership "is the ability to impress the will of the leader on those led and

[4] Sam Sawyer, S.J., "What meeting Pope Francis taught me about pastoral care," *America, The Jesuit Review*, December 15, 2022, accessed July 30, 2024, https://www.americamagazine.org/faith/2022/12/15/pastoral-mystery-many-things-244334.

[5] George Aschenbrenner, *The Hidden Self Grown Strong* (Institute for Priestly Formation, 2018), 32.

induce obedience, respect, loyalty, and cooperation."[6] Changing times and cultural makeup have led to a continual reevaluation of what leadership means. In 2010, Peter Northouse, a pioneer in leadership development, offered a very different definition of leadership as "a process whereby an individual influences a group of individuals to achieve a common goal."[7] This process highlights the leader's charismatic and collaborative effort, in contrast to the previously suggested authoritarian approach.

Similar changes in our understanding of leadership can be seen in the Church, especially as we have moved from a more clerical and authoritarian approach to Vatican II's more biblical approach focused on the "people of God." The essence of leadership today gravitates more toward "love for" and "service to" those whom one leads. The more aware leaders are about their own values, judgments, and biases, the better they are able to understand and empower others. Mother Teresa was famous for saying that her ministry was about "doing something beautiful for God." For her, what is

> **"True leadership is a matter of the heart; it is about being other-centered."**

essential in serving God is finding Christ and the dignity of life in every human being. In serving the poor, she served Christ. That was her theology of both pastoral care, and of leadership.

"True leadership is a matter of the heart," said Bob Briner and Ray Pritchard.[8] It is about being other-centered. One of the popular leadership styles in both ministerial and contemporary settings is the Servant Leadership model described by Robert Greenleaf.[9] Greenleaf was known for asking the question, "Do those served grow as persons? Do they, while being served, become healthier, wiser, freer, more autonomous, more likely to become servants?"[10] Here the leader models the way for his followers by being other-centered, helping them become better versions of themselves. The goal of seminary formation is just that: the growth of the seminarians we serve. They, in turn, model that experience for the parishioners they serve.

As Pope Francis said,

For leadership, there is only one road: service. There is no other way. If you have many qualities, [such as] the ability to communicate, etc., but you are not a servant, your leader-

---

[6] Bruce V. Moore, "The May Conference on Leadership," *Personnel Journal 6* (1927): 124-28, quoted in: Bernice M. Ledbetter, et al., *Reviewing Leadership: A Christian Evaluation of Current Approaches* (Baker Academic, 2004, 2016), 5.

[7] Peter G. Northouse, *Leadership: Theory and Practice* (Sage Publications, CA, 2000), 3.

[8] Bob Briner and Ray Pritchard, *Leadership Lessons from Jesus* (B&H Publishing Group, 1997, 1998), 228.

[9] Ronald L. Dufresne, et al., "Contributing to an Ignatian Perspective on Leadership," *The Journal of Jesuit Business Education* (2013), 8.

[10] Robert K. Greenleaf, "What is Servant Leadership?" *Greenleaf Center for Servant Leadership*, accessed August 8, 2024, https://www.greenleaf.org/what-is-servant-leadership/.

ship will fail. It is useless; it has no power to gather [people] together... Leadership must enter into service but with a personal love for the people.[11]

The characteristics of service are present in the secular as well as in the spiritual world. Simon Sinek, a well-known leadership speaker in the corporate sector, said, "The role of the leader is not to be in charge but to take care of those in his charge."[12] The pastoral leader's role is to take care of the spiritual and pastoral needs of the parish community.

## Attributes of Secular and Spiritual Leadership

In 1825, John Quincy Adams noted that, "If your actions inspire others to dream more, learn more, do more, and become more, you are a leader."[13] This is consistent with Greenleaf's definition of leadership and can only be accomplished through self-reflection resulting in increased awareness on the impact one's leadership has on others. Leadership is relational, and its outcomes are shaped by the mutual influence between the leader and their collaborators. This is true in both secular and spiritual settings.

According to the Center for Creative Leadership, effective leaders balance characteristics such as compassion, integrity, collaboration, effective communication, and resiliency; they are strategic and vision-focused. Effective leadership and effective communication are intertwined. [14]

In a spiritual setting, agapeic love is the foundation of pastoral leadership. Humility, listening, and compassion are at the heart both of agapeic love and of pastoral care. In many ways, the leadership model of today's pastor mirrors the example of Jesus. However, just as Jesus spoke, taught, and led in a manner appropriate to his time, today's pastor must also adapt to contemporary culture, ensuring that the Gospel remains consistent yet adaptable.

## Where Pastoral Care and Contemporary Leadership Intersect

> "Healthy secular and pastoral leadership styles both emphasize relational and collaborative qualities."

Healthy secular and pastoral leadership styles both emphasize relational and collaborative qualities. Key attributes in these

---

[11] Francis, "Address of Pope Francis to Rectors and Students of the Pontifical Colleges and Residences of Rome," *Vatican Website*, May 12, 2014, accessed July 30, 2024, https://www.vatican.va/content/francesco/en/speeches/2014/may/documents/papa-francesco_20140512_pontifici-collegi-convitti.html.

[12] Simon Sinek, "The Real Job of a Leader," *Live2Lead*, YouTube Video, August 22, 2022, accessed August 3, 2024. https://www.youtube.com/watch?v=48JfiFSp-kM, 00:15.

[13] Hannah L. Miller, (John Quincy Adams quoted in) "78 Leadership Quotes to Inspire Leaders", *Leaders*, October 6, 2023, accessed July 30, 2024, https://leaders.com/articles/leadership/leadership-quotes/.

[14] Micela Leis, "12 Essential Qualities of Effective Leadership," *Center for Creative Leadership*, July 3, 2024, accessed August 9, 2024, https://www.ccl.org/articles/leading-effectively-articles/characteristics-good-leader/.

areas include clear communication, active listening, empathy, respect, and teamwork. Additionally, one must adapt to one's environment – since in a multicultural world, the concept of respect can vary greatly among different cultures.

Where pastoral leadership differs from secular leadership is primarily in the realm of faith. A pastor's life must be imbued with God's love as he ministers to others. Similarly, those involved in seminary formation – whether as professors or formators – must minister in faith both with and to the seminarians. The Church's most effective leadership combines the best practices from both pastoral and secular leadership practices. While both styles aim to inspire and guide others, they do so from different perspectives and with distinct goals.

## Theology of Leadership: Christ-centered, Scripture-based

The theology of leadership begins with the recognition that the ministry of care is a calling which entails character transformation. Through this transformation, one becomes aware of the need for grace and recognizes that all is gift. With this awareness, one is ready to serve others, knowing that the ultimate goal of each act of service is to serve God.

Leadership is a decision one makes to serve others with integrity, compassion, and love. Pope Francis says, "A leader is good if he can generate other leaders among the young. If he only wants to be the sole leader, he is a tyrant... If they [leaders] do not

> **"Leadership is a decision one makes to serve others with integrity, compassion, and love."**

sow leadership in others, they are of no use; they are dictators."[15]

## Attributes of an Effective Leader

People often confuse the roles of leaders and managers. There is a significant difference between the role of a manager and that of a leader. "To manage means to accomplish activities and master routines, whereas to lead means to influence others and create vision for change."[16] Resilience, integrity, strategic visioning, and conflict resolution are some characteristics that distinguish a leader from a manager. "A leader does the right thing, while a manager does things right."[17] We need both leaders and managers in an effective organization.

But how do we teach leadership attributes to seminarians? Such teaching requires a profound

---

[15] Francis, "Via Satellite Video Conference With 'Scholas Occurrentes' Hosted By CNN," *Vatican Website*, September 17, 2015, accessed July 30, 2024, https://www.vatican.va/content/francesco/en/speeches/2015/september/documents/papa-francesco_20150917_scholas-occurrentes.html.

[16] Peter G. Northouse, *Theory and Practice of Leadership* (Sage, 2016), 14. Adapted from: J. P. Kotter, *A Force for Change. How Leadership Differs from Management* (New York: Free Press, 1990), 3-8.

[17] Peter G. Northouse, *Theory and Practice of Leadership* (Sage, 2016),14.

self-awareness and trust in the work of the Holy Spirit. "Leadership is a relationship of trust where commitments flow from character."[18] Nowhere is this truer than in pastoral ministry.

Teaching is one of the critical roles entrusted to priests. In his book, *The Courage to Teach*, Parker Palmer said, "We teach who we are."[19] The students connect with the teacher and then the subject. "Teaching is always done at the dangerous intersection of personal and public life. Good teaching cannot be reduced to technique; good teaching comes from the identity and integrity of the teacher."[20]

Kouzes and Posner suggest five essential attributes of an effective leader: "Modeling the way, inspiring a shared vision, challenging the process, enabling others to act, and encouraging the heart."[21] These attributes require a leader to be humble and self-aware.

Yet, while the spiritual health of the priest is the foundation of his being an effective pastoral leader, it is not sufficient. "It is not enough for a parish priest to be personally *holy*; he must also be *good* at his three basic ministries, *[Prophet]* teacher of the Word, *[Priest]* minister of the celebration of the Sacraments, and *[King]* leader of the faith community."[22] These three important roles model the way for their community in prayer, inspire them through a shared vision, challenge them to trust the process of choosing Christ in the world, and inspire them to become heart-centered by building relationships in the community. "Spiritual leadership is the ability to influence people to move from where they are to where God wants them to be through invitation, persuasion, example, and skillful use of the Church's rites, rituals, and rules."[23]

Today, a priest is responsible for both the spiritual care and the leadership of his community. Pastoral studies in the seminary must include the fundamentals of both skill sets, equipping seminarians to be confident in their ability to lead a parish community. "With good leadership, we flourish; without it, we flounder; with the wrong kind, we suffer."[24]

In leadership literature and research, one finds many thoughtful opinions about the most important characteristics of leadership, and everyone has their own particular preferences. Based on my personal and professional experience and research, I believe that the key characteristics of effective leaders today, whether in the secular or

---

[18] Walter C. Wright, *Relational Leadership: A Biblical Model for Influence and Service* (InterVarsity Press, 2000, 2009), 134.

[19] Parker Palmer, *The Courage to Teach: Exploring the Inner Landscape of a Teacher's Life* (Jossey-Bass Publishers, San Francisco, 1998), 1.

[20] *Ibid*, 17.

[21] Posner, et al., *The Leadership Challenge: How to Make Extraordinary Things Happen in Organizations* (HB Printing, San Francisco, CA, 2012), 15.

[22] Ronald Knott, *The Spiritual Leadership of a Parish Priest* (Sophronismos Press, Kentucky, 2007), 45.

[23] Ronald Knott, "From Designated Spiritual Leaders to Real Spiritual Leaders: The Challenge Facing Initial Priestly Formation," *Seminary Journal* (Spring 2011), 21.

[24] Bernice M. Ledbetter, *Reviewing Leadership: A Christian Evaluation of Current Approaches, 2nd Ed.* (Baker Academic, 2004, 2016), 1.

pastoral roles, include being skilled communicators, self-aware, relationship oriented, strategic visionaries, and people of integrity.

All leaders need to have a vision of something they wish to accomplish. For pastoral leaders, this may be summarized as the Kingdom of God, a world guided by and lived in the way of Christ, as understood by Scripture and Tradition. Effective priestly leaders must be able to communicate this vision in a variety of ways that are meaningful to their community. The pastor, whether as teacher or preacher, must have the necessary skills to break open the Word, to inspire, and to guide his flock. And as Vatican II reminds us, we must make use of modern means of communication, which in contemporary society may include social media, music, and the translation of the Gospel into media more accessible to contemporary cultures.[25] Importantly, leaders also cannot be effective without knowing themselves, their strengths and weaknesses, their biases and preferences.

The goal of self-awareness is to protect us from the worst in us and to accentuate the best in us. Closely related to self-awareness is being other-centered or relationship oriented. The fundamental nature of the Triune God is relationship, as Father, Son, and Spirit are three yet one, only to be fully experienced and understood in relationship to one another. Pastoral leaders, even more than secular leaders, must understand, empathize with, and care about their flock. For without this orientation of sincere empathy, how will those to whom they minister follow and be inspired? How will they be able to trust and be vulnerable? Leaders need to be strategic, not reactive and short-term driven. Thinking strategically means planning in such a way that actions taken contribute to moving toward the vision, inspiring the community to move together most effectively toward common goals. In this way, setbacks and squabbles are not allowed to distract anyone or cause leaders to take their eyes off the proverbial prize. Finally, leaders must be people of integrity. This doesn't mean leaders must be perfect. Being persons of integrity means their being committed to aligning external behaviors to internal values, even as they realize that being human means they will fall short. Acknowledging brokenness never excuses one from striving toward greater integrity, which is why the Sacrament of Reconciliation is so important to our spirituality. In celebrating this sacrament, we recognize our human frailty, while opening ourselves to the ever-greater grace of God.

> **"With good leadership, we flourish; without it, we flounder; with the wrong kind, we suffer."**

These leadership characteristics are crucial for both secular and pastoral leaders, though they may manifest differently in each

---

25 Second Vatican Council, "'Communio Et Progressio' On The Means of Social Communication," *Vatican Website*, accessed September 21, 2024, https:// vatican.va/ roman_curia/pontifical_councils/pccs/documents/rc_pc_pccs_doc_23051971_communio_en.html.

context. Effective pastoral formation programs aim to develop leaders who embody these traits. Good pastoral formation that integrates solid theological education with practical field experience will develop pastors who not only exhibit these characteristics but also commit to ongoing development throughout their lives.

## The Current Climate in Which Pastors Find Themselves

Pastoral formation programs in the United States have changed over the years. In the past, seminaries often relied on pastors to provide practical education to the newly ordained priests. In this context, mentoring pastors highlighted the ministerial skills that priests needed, providing feedback and training through role modeling. In that model of formation, the recently ordained received several pastoral assignments that offer them opportunities to experience various leadership styles and parish communities under the supervision of experienced pastors. Today, the transition into ministry is a special challenge because social and cultural changes have shaped contemporary America in powerful ways. Both the time spent preparing for the ministry and the transition environment have changed significantly.

Today, the newly ordained often have less than two years of ministry before they are given the responsibilities of a pastorate, and sometimes not just one but multiple parishes. Most frequently, the newly ordained today have few opportunities to learn from the modeling of a mentor-pastor and respond to their example and their guidance before themselves becoming pastors.

In addition, the Church of today is simply not our grandparents' Church. "Growing up in the Church in the 1990's wasn't what it is today," notes Jonathan Cerda, a seminarian in First-Theology studying for the Archdiocese of Baltimore. "Not just the 'One in Being with the Father' or 'I am not worthy to receive you' but the music was also different at the time."[26] In the past, many seminarians and priests came from European backgrounds and were often in cultural alignment with the immigrant populations they served. Today, international candidates who hail from Africa, Asia, Southeast Asia, and South America will often be serving communities with different cultural heritages. Moreover, due to the declining number of both parishioners and pastors, many parishes have consolidated. In any parish, the laity can range from being highly educated, both theologically and academically, to lacking formal educational background in either area. Thus, the new pastor can face many challenges in parish management and parishioner engagement.

The impact of social media and globalization also cannot be underestimated. Even parish

---

[26] Jonathan Cerda, First-Theology Seminarian, Archdiocese of Baltimore, *Nostalgia: Theological Reflection*, September 19, 2024, 1.(Printed with permission)

boundaries, which used to be normative and helped to define community, are often not observed (except for some requirements in canon law), making it challenging at times for even the most experienced pastor to navigate issues of parish identity and cultural diversity. Naturally, the trend toward more parish mergers has exacerbated the complexity.

Therefore, seminaries must take these societal and local community changes into consideration in their formation program, as uncomfortable and paradigm-shifting as their impact may be. The formation of priests must be dynamic if they are to proclaim the gospel effectively in today's world. The gospel is both always the same and ever new, a part of that newness being that it is shared and received in contemporary "languages." Fr. James D. Proffitt, the Vicar for Clergy of the Archdiocese of Baltimore, put it succinctly; "It is not that the [older] priests are not competent. It's that the church they were trained to pastor is not the church that we are in now."[27] The mission and values of the Church haven't changed, but the cultural context has made the practice of ministry more complex.

## The Sulpician Model of Training Pastoral Leaders at St. Mary's Seminary

The purpose of pastoral formation is for the seminarian to learn and understand how to be a shepherd imbued with the charity of Christ, filled with a missionary spirit, and possessing pastoral competence. Pastoral skills are developed through formative, supervised experiences in ministry and reflection upon those experiences.[28]

The Society of St. Sulpice, dedicated to priestly formation in the United States since 1791, began in Paris. Its founder, Fr. Jean-Jacques Olier, established a seminary and a community of priests in 1641 and began the Society of the Priests of St. Sulpice in 1642.

St. Mary's Seminary was opened in Baltimore in 1791, with four Sulpicians and five students, creating the first Catholic institution of higher learning to open in the U.S. In 1822, Pope Pius VII gave St. Mary's the right to grant ecclesiastical degrees, the first Catholic institution in the U.S. to be given that distinction.[29]

> **"The Sulpician model, as developed at St. Mary's, is giving seminarians the tools to continue learning and growing throughout their priesthood."**

The Sulpician tradition of priestly formation is built on the five core values of the Society of the Priest of St. Sulpice: a commitment to the priesthood, the cultivation of an apostolic spirit, an emphasis on spiritual formation, the creation of formational community, and the exercise of

---

[27] George P. Matysek, Jr., "Evangelization At Heart," *Catholic Review Vol 89* (June 2024), 24.

[28] PPF, no. 394.

[29] Society of St. Sulpice, Province of the United States, "*Sulpician History*," accessed August 8, 2024, http://sulpicians.org/who-we-are/history/.

collegiality. These core values are built into St. Mary's formation process, as well as being found in the vision of *Pastores Dabo Vobis (PDV)*, John Paul II's landmark document on priestly formation and in the *Program of Priestly Formation* (PPF, hereafter). *Pastores Dabo Vobis* states that,

> The Priesthood, along with the Word of God and the sacramental signs which it serves, belongs to the constitutive elements of the Church. The priest's ministry is entirely on behalf of the Church; it aims to promote the exercise of the common priesthood of the entire People of God.[30]

At St. Mary's, our formation program prepares seminarians to be ministers of the Word and sacraments through studies and field experiences. Fourth Century Church Father Gregory Nazianzus said,

> We must begin by purifying ourselves; we must be instructed to be able to instruct, become light to illuminate, draw close to God to bring him close to others, be sanctified to sanctify, lead by the hand, and counsel prudently. It is not enough that one be emotionally and spiritually mature, these attributes must be placed at the service of others in ministry.[31]

This is the goal of seminary formation in a nutshell.

## An Overview of St. Mary's Pastoral Formation Philosophy

At St. Mary's, we make formation intentional by designing every course with a defined pastoral purpose and an expressed pastoral outcome. Professors demonstrate how theological insights and doctrinal truths animate the journey of parish communities to meet life's demands.

In this model, St. Mary's is the center for the seminarians' human, intellectual, spiritual, and pastoral formation. The parishes, hospitals, and direct service sites are the learning labs. The PPF states

> Pastoral formation depends greatly on the quality of supervision. To serve as a supervisor of seminarians calls for experience, competence, and generosity. Priests and others who serve as supervisors, mentors, and professors are an extension of the seminary.[32]

At all formation levels, the quality of supervision is a critical element of our pastoral formation program. Classroom studies, supervised ministry, and theological and pastoral reflections, along with community living, liturgy, and

---

[30] John Paul II, "Post-Synodal Apostolic Exhortation: Pastores Dabo Vobis," *Vatican Website*, March 15, 1992, accessed July 30, 2024, https://www.vatican.va/content/john-paul-ii/en/apost_exhortations/documents/hf_jp-ii_exh_25031992_pastores-dabo-vobis.html, 16.

[31] Mike Aquilina, *Friendship and the Fathers: How the Early Church Evangelized* (Emmaus Road Publishing, OH, 2021), 122.

[32] PPF, no. 371.

weekly practice of Sulpician meditation, come together to create a formational community (*communauté éducatrice*).

All seminarians are required to spend time in supervised placements. These placements challenge the seminarians to personal growth and greater self-understanding. What has been studied in the classroom comes alive in these supervised settings. Through these integrated and intentional experiences, key leadership characteristics and skills are nurtured. Our program equips those who will be pastors to evangelize effectively in contemporary culture. The skills they learn will help them evangelize and catechize the diverse communities entrusted to their care.

In the supervised ministry settings, seminarians are immersed in an experiential setting where they learn and grow in their human, intellectual, spiritual, and pastoral competencies.

## Graduated Ministry Opportunities

Our pastoral internships are graduated ministry opportunities that build on each other – as the seminarian moves from one level of formation to the next. There are five steps in pastoral formation, and each level focuses on different aspects of pastoral ministry and the development of particular skills.

The chart (above right) describes the class levels and competencies.

The Five Steps in Pastoral Formation*

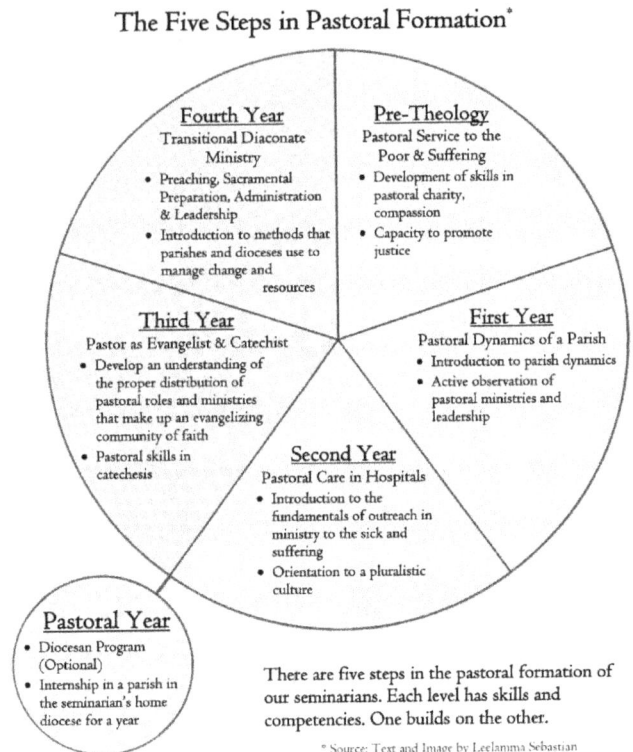

**Fourth Year**
Transitional Diaconate Ministry
- Preaching, Sacramental Preparation, Administration & Leadership
- Introduction to methods that parishes and dioceses use to manage change and resources

**Pre-Theology**
Pastoral Service to the Poor & Suffering
- Development of skills in pastoral charity, compassion
- Capacity to promote justice

**Third Year**
Pastor as Evangelist & Catechist
- Develop an understanding of the proper distribution of pastoral roles and ministries that make up an evangelizing community of faith
- Pastoral skills in catechesis

**First Year**
Pastoral Dynamics of a Parish
- Introduction to parish dynamics
- Active observation of pastoral ministries and leadership

**Second Year**
Pastoral Care in Hospitals
- Introduction to the fundamentals of outreach in ministry to the sick and suffering
- Orientation to a pluralistic culture

**Pastoral Year**
- Diocesan Program (Optional)
- Internship in a parish in the seminarian's home diocese for a year

There are five steps in the pastoral formation of our seminarians. Each level has skills and competencies. One builds on the other.

\* Source: Text and Image by Leelamma Sebastian

Our pre-theology program assists the seminarian in learning about who he is and how he responds to people and situations as he ministers.

To establish appropriate goals for the year, the seminarian creates a learning agreement outlining three to five objectives, each focused on enhancing charity, compassion, and social justice awareness. The supervisor provides both informal feedback and formal evaluation on a seminarian's professional and personal strengths, as well as on areas that need improvement. This feedback, along with the seminarian's theological reflection paper, is incorporated into his formation report. All seminarians participate in facilitated, small-group theological and pastoral reflection sessions, offering a forum in which to reflect, share, and receive feedback.

Pre-theology seminarian Joseph Lewis, from the Diocese of Wilmington, Delaware, shared how profoundly impacted he was by his experience at a direct service site for people with developmental disabilities:

Reflecting on my experiences during this year's ministry … brings to mind a narrative of development and community. First, my own self-development as I engaged people who might be considered the 'least among the flock' and how I had to overcome an initial feeling of uncertainty and unease to connect and communicate. Secondly, community amongst all of God's children as I witnessed the joyful interactions of people who cannot function independently but have learned to rely on others. Throughout this assignment, I learned to adapt, innovate, and relate to various brothers and sisters who live in very different circumstances. From this, I was able to engage the community in the pastoral and human dimensions as well as spiritual. God is ever-present. He is with those residents who struggle to live day-to-day. He is with those who are humbled in heart and eager to help others. And He has been with my teammate and me as we faced uncertainty that led to really gracious moments of ministering to a community that desperately needs a little hope and love.[33]

Still applying classroom learning can be challenging due to the unpredictability of ministry settings. A key characteristic of good leadership is to be other-centered. This trait is enhanced by deepening one's sense of compassion and empathy through service to others.

First, Third, and Fourth Theology formation are all centered around the parish learning team, which I will discuss in detail below, after comments about Second Theology.

During Second Theology, seminarians serve in healthcare ministries. This year focuses on human formation helping them to understand more about themselves and how this self-awareness influences the way they serves others. The seminarians' hospital assignments are concurrent with pastoral care and practice and medical ethics classes, which helps them as they apply practical skills, such as active listening and the ministry of presence. Because we are a culture of doers, the ability to be present without doing something more can be challenging for many, yet this practical approach allows them to be present without having to fix issues. The onsite supervisor accompanies the seminarian as he learns to sit with the discomfort he might feel in those situations and helps him to process what is happening within himself. This activity is a tremendous help for future priests as they will soon move into ministering to sick individuals and their families in their parishes who are experiencing grief.

---

[33] Joseph Lewis, Pre-Theology Seminarian, Diocese of Wilmington, *Spring Theological Reflection*, April 29, 2024,1. (Printed with permission)

As seminarian Louis Castrillon, from the Archdiocese of Baltimore, Maryland, reflected, on his ministry visit with a patient:

> During my hospital visit, I found a profound connection between my assignment experience and my faith ... upon reflection, I realized that my interaction with the patient in the hospital was a transformative lesson in the unexpected ways God moves and communicates His love through us. It reaffirmed the impact of spiritual care and challenged me to cultivate a deeper reliance on God's strength in my service, fostering both humility and a renewed passion for my ministry.[34]

The hospital ministry experience can be very intense, as seminarians encounter very ill people, those facing their own death or the death of a loved one, and the elderly; seeing very sick children, for example, can potentially create questions regarding God's compassion and raise the proverbial question, "Why?" These are the kinds of experiences that will lead seminarians to develop important skills of self-awareness, praying with someone who is from a different faith or cultural background, and being other-centered.

At St. Mary's each parish learning team consists of three seminarians, one each from First-year, Third-year, and Fourth-year (transitional deacons), and each team is assigned to a parish in the Archdiocese of Baltimore. The seminarians work together as a team of three, with the transitional deacon (Fourth-year seminarian) serving as the team leader. In this model, the parish becomes the learning lab for the team that integrates classroom learning of inquiry (First-year), teaching (Third-year), and liturgical, sacramental, and leadership skills (the transitional deacon). The First-year seminarians concentrate on actively observing the ministries and dynamics of the parish, posing questions such as why the pastor is effective and what makes the parish community vibrant. He brings these questions to the small group reflection sessions to process them with his group. The Third-year seminarian focuses on teaching catechesis and on understanding his role as a public person. The transitional deacon's primary ministry is liturgical and sacramental, with the pastor serving as his supervisor. As the team leader, the transitional deacon coordinates communication with the pastor regarding ministry activities and supports his team as needed. This role offers the transitional deacon an opportunity to develop leadership skills.

Thomas Dzwonczyk, a deacon from the Diocese of Scranton, Pennsylvania, shared how he was inspired by young students and their heartfelt spiritual experience:

> ...I had the great joy of teaching many CCD classes and leading some of the younger students in Eucharistic Adoration. I was skeptical about Adoration, because I thought

---

[34] Luis Castrillon, Second Theology Seminarian, Archdiocese of Baltimore, *Spring Theological Reflection*, April 28, 2024, 1.

the children would talk throughout. Who am I to underestimate the Lord? The kids greatly enjoyed it. It was my own faith which was shown to be deficient in this instance. There were many weekends at the parish when I 'just served Mass.' But heaven forbid I ever adopt such a minimalist attitude! Indeed, there will be many days where I just 'celebrate Mass.' The Mass must always remain at the center of the priest's existence. If the Mass loses priority in the priest's heart, then the priest is sure to deviate from the Lord's will. In times of doubt or uncertainty, I am always edified by the people's faith. Their commitment to the Lord in a world that does anything but support religion is truly admirable. Jesus said, 'Where two or three are gathered in my name, I am there among them.' Where better to experience this reality than the parish? Lord, send me![35]

The onsite ministry experiences can both challenge and inspire seminarians to be fully present, yet reflecting on these experiences with their mentors helps highlight areas of growth and identify areas needing improvement.

The Pastoral Year Internship program is an optional diocesan-based initiative that allows seminarians to spend a year immersed in parish ministry within their diocese. This experience provides an excellent opportunity to get to know the presbyterate in their home diocese, to further discern their vocation to the priesthood, and to become familiar with various parish ministries. During this year, they are also introduced to the interconnectedness of the diocese, its parishes, and their parochial schools.

Still, even with the best classroom instruction, seminarians don't receive all the essential skills needed for on-site ministry. To bridge this gap, we invite experts from various fields to conduct workshops that offer additional resources and practical skills for real world situations. These workshops are tailored to each class and level of formation, covering topics such as Giving and Receiving Feedback, Pastoral Communications, the Evangelizing Parish, the Ministry of Presence, Pastoral Charity, and Priestly Wellness.

In addition, each year we invite three recently ordained priests to participate in a panel discussion with the Fourth-year theology class. This allows the transitional deacons to hear from recent alumni and to ask questions about their experiences, including the surprises and learning moments they encountered as they transitioned.

At the ministry sites, seminarians apply their insights from the classroom into practice through faith-in-action. Through small group theological and pastoral reflections sessions, we support seminarians in processing and learning from their field ministry experiences. These cohort groups consisting of five seminarians each and are accompanied by a facilitator who may

---

[35] Thomas Dzwonczyk, Transitional Deacon, Diocese of Scranton, *Fall Theological Reflection*, November 4, 2024, 2. (Printed with permission)

include St. Mary's faculty and priests from the Archdiocese of Baltimore. This reflective process allows seminarians to discuss with their facilitators and peers how their on-site experiences are deepening their formation. Through pastoral reflections, they learn from the collective wisdom of the group, adding valuable skills to their toolbox. Group sharing helps seminarians to connect with their emotions, bridging the gap between the brain and the heart.

To ensure ongoing evaluation and assessment of the program, we depend heavily on the feedback from the seminarians and their field supervisors. At the end of each semester, seminarians write a reflection paper that describes their field ministry experiences and how these experiences have influenced their formation. Another assessment tool for the Fourth-year (transitional deacons) is the written rating of their homilies provided by the pastor and the parishioners. Feedback, formal and informal, from parishes, pastors, and seminarians themselves, provide valuable insights into a seminarian's progress and into the

> **"The characteristics of good leaders – being strategic visionaries, skilled communicators, relationship – oriented, and men of integrity and self-aware – are developed in each level of formation, and in the Fourth-year (transitional diaconate year) they all come together."**

effectiveness of ministry environments. We use these reports to assess our program's success and to make necessary adjustments.

Once a semester, our seminarians are formally evaluated by their ministry supervisors, who celebrate their strengths and provide recommendations for improvement. This feedback is incorporated into the faculty formation report for the bishops. To express our gratitude and to celebrate our collaboration with the ministry sites, once a year, we invite the pastoral ministry supervisors to join the community for a feedback session, evening prayer, reception, and dinner.

The characteristics of good leaders – being strategic visionaries, skilled communicators, relationship – oriented, and men of integrity and self-aware – are developed in each level of formation, and in the Fourth-year (transitional diaconate year) they all come together. The table below (page 58) outlines the skills and competencies that pastoral leaders integrate at St. Mary's to become effective in their respective formation levels.

**Conclusion**

The fundamental role of seminary formation is to develop pastoral leaders. This process necessitates collaboration among the seminary educators and ministry supervisors who interact with the seminarians. Feedback from the supervisors, and the seminarians' theological and pastoral reflections allow the seminary formators to evaluate the effectiveness of our program. However, it is unrealistic to think that seminary education and formation will cover all that a seminarian needs in his future ministry.

The goal of seminary education is to prepare well-rounded priests who can effectively lead and serve their communities, exemplifying their love for God in their relationship with others. Spiritual and pastoral leadership are inherently relational and inseparable. Our program at St. Mary's combines the concepts of pastoral care and secular leadership to provide ministry leadership experiences in order that today's future priests will learn to lead like the "Good Shepherd."

While human formation is the foundation of priestly identity, being a prayerful person is necessary but not sufficient to become a spiritual shepherd. That is why insights from secular leadership research are invaluable, and their integration into pastoral formation enhances the development of well-rounded pastors.

Understandably, those in formation may sometimes feel they are under constant scrutiny and must "perform" for their formators and faculty. In fact, this couldn't be further from the truth. The primary goal of the evaluations in the formation program is to cultivate the best qualities in our seminarians, enabling them to follow in the footsteps of our Good Shepherd.

Following the Sulpician model, St. Mary's seminary program aims to develop Christ-centered, collegial, and community-focused men committed to the priesthood with an apostolic spirit to serve the Church in the ministry of love. Learning pastoral leadership in the classroom is also essential for preparing future priests, but it is not sufficient. In order for the seminarians to learn pastoral leadership and (for seminary faculty to teach it), one needs; a holistic approach that includes theological knowledge, spiritual formation, practical skills and experience, engagement with contemporary research, and character development. Yet another critical component in maintaining his own healthy spiritual care is how a seminarian nurtures his interior life. The Sulpician charism of commitment to priesthood, spiritual formation, collegiality, and community living celebrates and encourages the growth of healthy relationships and leadership skills as the seminarians enter into parish life.

The Sulpician model, as developed at St. Mary's, is giving seminarians the tools to continue learning and growing throughout their priesthood while adapting creatively and joyfully to the changing circumstances they will inevitably encounter in their service of the people of God in the ministry of love.

Leelamma Sebastian, M.A., M.S.C.P.
Leelamma Sebastian is Director of Pastoral Formation at St. Mary's Seminary & University.

## Evaluation and Integration: Ministry Toward Leadership*

### Benchmarks, Evaluations & Leadership Skills

| | Pre-Theology | First Year | Second Year | Pastoral Year | Third Year | Fourth Year ** |
|---|---|---|---|---|---|---|
| **Pastoral Ministry Theme** | Service to the Poor & Suffering | Dynamics of a Parish | Pastoral Care in Health Care | Diocesan Program (Optional) | Pastor as Catechist & Evangelist | Pastoral Leadership |
| **Benchmarks** | Skills in charity and compassion<br><br>Capacity to promote justice<br><br>Ability to minister to people from all walks of life | Understanding of basic parish dynamics through active inquiry<br><br>Knowledge of pastoral ministries and leadership via observation | Demonstrated capacity to be comfortable in uncomfortable situations<br><br>Skilled outreach to the sick and their families<br><br>Ability to engage with a pluralistic culture | Successful internship in a parish in the seminarian's home diocese for a year | Understanding the unique role of the priest in the context of other ministries in an evangelizing community<br><br>Skills in catechesis and teaching Scripture and Tradition to all age groups | Competency in preaching, sacramental preparation, and basic administration<br><br>Capacity to articulate the methods that parishes and dioceses use to manage change and resource utilization |
| **Evaluation** | Informal feedback and formal evaluation from supervisor demonstrating increased awareness in charity, social justice, and compassion<br><br>Seminarian's theological reflection papers align with the supervisor's report<br><br>Facilitated theological and pastoral reflection sessions at the seminary with fellow seminarians | Informal feedback and formal evaluation from supervisor demonstrating growth in ministry, including demonstration of initiative in learning, and active interaction with parishioners, staff, and pastor<br><br>Seminarian's theological reflection papers align with the supervisor's report<br><br>Facilitated theological and pastoral reflection sessions at the seminary with fellow seminarians | Individual and team reflection with the chaplain / supervisor<br><br>Formal evaluation from supervisor<br><br>Seminarian's theological reflection papers align with the supervisor's report<br><br>Facilitated theological and pastoral reflections at the seminary with fellow seminarians | The specific diocese determines this process<br><br>A report is shared with the seminary | Informal feedback and formal evaluation from supervisor demonstrating growth in ministry<br><br>Demonstrates the role of priest as teacher and evangelizer<br><br>Seminarian's theological reflection papers align with the supervisor's report<br><br>Facilitated theological and pastoral reflections at the seminary with fellow seminarians | Informal feedback and formal evaluations from the pastor on ministry, interaction with parishioners, and parish learning team<br><br>Meetings with the team, providing feedback and addressing conflict, and engaging in effective communication among members, seminary faculty, and his pastoral supervisor<br><br>Seminarian's theological reflection papers align with the supervisor's report<br><br>Facilitated theological and pastoral reflections at the seminary with fellow seminarians |
| **Leadership Qualities Addressed** | Self-awareness<br><br>Integrity | Skilled Communicator<br><br>Relationship Oriented | Self-awareness<br><br>Integrity<br><br>Skilled Communicator | Dependent upon the diocesan program | Skilled Communicator<br><br>Integrity<br><br>Relationship Oriented | **Strategic Visionary ***<br><br>**Skilled Communicator ***<br><br>**Relationship Oriented ***<br><br>Integrity<br><br>Self-awareness<br><br>* All leadership qualities are evident but these are emphasized. |

* Source: Image and Text by Leelamma Sebastian

** Usually Transitional Deacons

# Preparing Foreign-Born Seminarians for the US Church

## Hy Nguyen, P.S.S., M.A., S.T.D.

## Introduction

With priestly vocations in decline, the Church in the United States has recently become increasingly dependent on foreign-born priests for ministry. According to the CARA survey for early 2024, approximately 400 seminarians in the United States are expected to be ordained, with 80% being diocesan priests and 20% from religious orders. Of these, about 23% are foreign-born, a slight decrease from 26% in 2022. The majority of these seminarians come from Vietnam, Mexico, Colombia, and the Philippines.[1]

This article focuses on foreign-born seminarians studying in seminaries in the United States, rather than foreign-born priests who come to serve directly. While much of the discussion applies to foreign-born clergy, the primary focus is on the formulation of seminary training programs for these foreign-born seminarians.[2]

As the Chairman of the Formation Support for Vietnam (FSVN) and the "Ministries to the West" program, which connects U.S. dioceses with Vietnamese priestly candidates[3], I offer practical points to help form foreign-born seminarians for effective ministry in the United States.

> **"The U.S. Church has recently become increasingly dependent on foreign-born priests for ministry."**

## History

From its inception, the American Catholic Church has always been a "Church of immigrants," shaped profoundly by immigration more than any other single factor. Historically, immigrants have always faced significant challenges, including discrimination based on religion, culture, race and class. European Catholic immigrants of the early twentieth century often faced discrimination based on religion and class. Later on, Catholic immigrants from the "Third World" faced additional barriers tied to cultural and racial differences.

---

[1] *The Ordination Class of 2023 CARA study* can be found on the USCCB website.

[2] In 2006, Dean R. Hoge and Aniedi Okure published *International Priests in America: Challenges and Opportunities* (Liturgical Press, 2006), a report focusing on foreign-born priests who ministered in the U.S. from 1985 to 2005. Although some of the data and information in the book are now over 20 years old, the Church can still draw many valuable lessons and insights from the challenges discussed, which remain relevant today.

[3] The Formation Support for Vietnam (FSVN) is a non-profit organization that helps to bring priests, seminarians, and religious brothers and sisters from Vietnam to study in the United States, then returning to serve in Vietnam. Recently, the FSVN launched the "Ministries to the West" program, which helps young Vietnamese candidates pursue priestly vocations in US dioceses.

Recognizing these spiritual needs, the church has always found ways to care for immigrants, adapting its pastoral ministries over time to rise to the increasing challenges we face as a society.

In early times, ethnic groups were often served by ethnic priests who either accompanied immigrants to the U.S. or were later invited to serve specific communities. Ethnic parishes were built to respond to their own needs.[4]

By 1791, the Society of St. Sulpice priests founded St. Mary's Seminary and University in Baltimore, the first seminary in the United States, to train priests for the U.S. Church. However, the program was not initially designed to address cultural and linguistic diversity. It was simply designed to serve the Catholic Church.

In society, the image of the "melting pot" was promoted as a model for life in the new land, and therefore seminarians of all races were encouraged to assimilate with the dominant "American" culture.

Today, immigration continues to shape the World, as it does the Church. As of September 2023, the Pew Research Center reported that the US has approximately 47.8 million foreign-born Americans, about 14% of the total population.[5]

This is a common concern that needs to be addressed. While societal treatment and attitude toward immigrants can be harsh, the U.S. Church has become the essential source of support and assistance for many Catholic immigrants and refugees.

## Program of Priestly Formation[6] and Ratio Fundamentalis[7]

The *Program of Priestly Formation* (*PPF*6th ed.) provides guidance for seminaries in establishing formation programs. Although the *PPF* does not have specific guidelines for forming foreign-born seminarians,

> "Although the PPF does not have specific guidelines for forming foreign-born seminarians, the general guidelines are to form all seminarians for the multicultural Church, and the Church's concerns are to minister to the faithful fruitfully."

the general guidelines are to form all seminarians for the multicultural Church, and the Church's concerns are to minister to the faithful fruitfully. Based on what the Church wants us to do, I hope to suggest some appropriate applications for

---

[4] It was similar to a "personal perish" today, a parish established for a particular group of the same language and culture.

[5] The PEW Research noted that in 1970, the number of foreign-born people was only about a fifth of what it is today. The statistics can be found on the Census government webpage.

[6] *Program of Priestly Formation in the United States of America* (6th ed) was approved in June 2022 and published in January 2023 by the USCCB.

[7] *The Gift of the Priestly Vocation – Ratio Fundamentalis Institutionis Sacerdotalis* issued by the Congregation for the Clergy in December 2016, available on Vatican website.

forming foreign-born seminarians in the US seminaries.

Below are key points from the *PPF*:

Recognizing the present state of the church, *PPF* reminds us all to remain culturally diverse:

> a. The United States is a nation with a rich cultural heritage of freedom, equality, justice for the oppressed, and open dialogue... However...Catholic institutions are not immune to the persistence of racism in society.
>
> b. In most areas of the United States, the norm is a high level of cultural, linguistic, and economic diversity. Continued Catholic immigration has situated numerous newly arrived people... alongside numerous other Catholic laity who are native-born. (*PPF*, 20. a,b)

The *PPF* lends support to diversity in seminary admissions:

> Applicants from diverse ethnic and cultural backgrounds should be given every encouragement.... It is also important that applicants from other countries receive special help in gaining the necessary understanding of the religious and cultural context for priestly ministry and life in the United States. (*PPF*, 68).

Building multicultural seminary communities, the PPF says:

> The seminary community and individual seminarians should appreciate the presence of a multicultural, multiethnic, and international community within the seminary. This environment provides a mutually enriching dimension to a seminary community and reflects the realities of pastoral life awaiting seminarians. (*PPF*, 162)

**Cultivating human maturity in the seminary community, it says:**

> The human formation of men for the priesthood aims to prepare..... (g) A man who relates well with others, free of prejudice, and who is willing to work with people of diverse cultural backgrounds: A man capable of wholesome relations with women and men as relatives, friends, colleagues, staff members, and teachers and as people encountered in areas of apostolic work. (*PPF*, 183. g.)

Regarding liturgical diversity:

> Because the liturgical life of the seminary shapes the sensitivities and attitudes of seminarians for future ministry.... The seminary liturgy should also promote in seminarians a respect for legitimate, rubrically approved liturgical expressions of cultural diversity as well as the Church's ancient liturgical patrimony. (*PPF*, 248)

Adapting theological curricula for multicultural ministry, the PPF recommends:

> The theological curriculum... should address the unique needs of a multicultural society... (PPF, 357)
>
> [The] pastoral formation means more than acquiring skills... Effective ministry means... that enables the priest to relate to people across a number of different cultures and theological and ecclesial outlooks. Formators must help the seminarian put on both the mind and heart of Christ, the Good Shepherd, including exposing him to cultural and linguistic diversity. This exposure enables him to more fully welcome newcomers to the culturally rich society in which we live, while at the same time encouraging these newcomers to maintain the richness of their own cultural identity. (PPF, 370, d).

The PPF advocates for cultural competency:

> Priests serving in the United States, regardless of their cultural background, often serve in a multicultural setting. Working toward cultural competency, including language competency, to meet pastoral needs in his diocese should be part of the formation a seminarian receives during the propaedeutic stage, so as to lay a solid foundation for continued formation in cultural competency in later stages. (PPF, 373)

Ensuring appropriate pastoral placement and legal awareness, the PPF states:

> In his pastoral assignments,...the seminarian demonstrates pastoral charity in his sensitivity and prudence with behavior and language in pastoral settings. He demonstrates multicultural sensitivity and openness to people of all ages, religious backgrounds, and

**"The seminary community should appreciate the presence of a multicultural, multiethnic, and international community within the seminary." (PPF, 162)**

> social status in speech and action. He demonstrates the ability to collaborate with both men and women. He demonstrates the capacity to abide prudently by safe environment guidelines and to maintain proper boundaries in all relationships, especially with minors and other vulnerable individuals. (PPF, 377)
>
> The program should include placements in which seminarians will experience the richness and diversity of the various cultural, racial, and ethnic groups that compose the Catholic Church in the United States. Such placements can also

*provide opportunities to sharpen language skills. (PPF, 395)*

In the academic field, the PPF reminds us of faculty diversity and professional development:

*It is important to recruit well-trained and experienced professors from diverse ethnic, racial, and cultural backgrounds. (PPF, 475)*

*If the seminary has a multicultural community, the professors should be encouraged to participate in programs and workshops that acquaint them with the specific situation and formational needs of their seminarians. (PPF, 476)*

**Ratio Fundamentalis** instructs the issue of Vocations and Migrants:

*... It is important that Christian communities offer constant pastoral care of immigrant families that live and work in their country for a time... Vocations to the priestly ministry can arise from within these families, which must be accompanied, keeping in mind the need for a gradual cultural integration. (RF 26)*

*There are others who, feeling called by the Lord, leave their own country, in order to receive formation for the priesthood elsewhere. It is important to pay attention to their personal history and to the background from which they have come, and to assess carefully the motivations for their vocational choice, establishing a dialogue with their Church of origin whenever possible. In any case, during the process of formation it will be necessary to find ways and means to ensure an adequate integration, without underestimating the challenge of cultural differences, which can, at times, make vocational discernment rather complex. (RF 27)*

## Seminary Formation Preparation

To align with the directives of PPF, seminaries must work towards developing robust programs that thoroughly prepare foreign seminarians for future ministry. Key considerations include:

## Who Are They? Understanding the Foreign Seminarians

Foreign-born seminarians generally fall into one of two categories: those who arrived in the United States as teenagers, and those sponsored by dioceses directly from their home countries.

The first group arriving in the U.S. as teenagers most likely attended high school or college in the States. Although this group is more likely to speak English well, they are still considered the "betwixt and between", meaning they do not completely belong to any one world.[8] At home, they live by their own culture and speak their native language. At school or the workplace, they act accordingly in order to assimilate into "American" society.

> **"Seminaries must seek to understand the unique experiences and perspectives of foreign-born priests and take initiative to bridge the cultural gaps."**

The second group is those sponsored by dioceses to study in the United States, especially those who come directly from "third world" countries, and the seminary becomes their initial place of cultural refuge." This group faces significant linguistic and cultural challenges, experiencing cultural shock because everything is new and strange: food, eating habits, clothes, and greeting gestures, even transportation and communication. Along with the Mentor and the Spiritual Director who accompanies these people formally and periodically, the seminary should arrange a native companion to help guide them through the adjustment process.

**Integration challenges**

Seminaries have the responsibility to help foreign-born seminarians adjust and adapt to new cultures effectively and comfortably. To better orient candidates, seminaries must seek to understand the unique experiences and perspectives of foreign-born priests and take initiative to bridge the cultural gaps that present themselves in a diverse clergy.

> **"Language proficiency is the most important factor in assimilating to a new culture and is critical for effective ministry and social confidence."**

Workshops that educate the seminary community about other cultures are essential in avoiding common misconceptions while fostering deeper understanding. For example, the tendency to homogenize groups, such as assuming all South Americans (Mexicans, Hondurans, Colombians, Venezuelans...) or all Asian Americans (Vietnamese, Chinese, and Filipinos...) are the same is one discussion that must be had. These microaggressions and cultural misunderstandings can hinder growth as a community and ultimately distract the seminary from their true mission in serving the Catholic Church.

Language proficiency is the most important factor in assimilating to a new culture and is critical for effective ministry and social confidence. Seminaries need to have an ESL program or equivalent so that these seminarians can integrate quickly into their new life. First and

---

[8] The phrase "betwixt and between" means they are between the two worlds and belong neither here nor there. See Ronald Takaki, *Strangers from a Different Shore. A*

*History of Asian Americans* (New York: Penguin Books, 1989), 18.

foremost, language is the key that opens all other doors to their new life in America. In addition, the Accent Modification Program aims to assist with this issue, as a common complaint today from parishioners is that they do not understand foreign priests.

Integration is a lifelong process, and it requires a lot of effort. In addition to cultural and social understanding, foreign-born seminarians also need to understand the American Catholic culture in which they serve. For seminarians from Africa and Asia, exposure to women and the role of laity in the church needs to be appreciated. Many common things accepted in their countries may be considered clericalism and unacceptable in the US. Therefore, intensive workshops or programs are needed for this purpose.

## Intellectual Programs

Many foreign-born seminarians struggle with academic expectations and practices in the United States.

In my experience for example, many African and Asian seminarians are reluctant to engage in pedagogy in American universities. Some do not speak up in class because they are not used to questioning their professors or authorities. Furthermore, the curriculum in many places relies

> **"It is very important to help foreign-born seminarians have a basic knowledge of the laws of the United States to avoid unintentional violations."**

on knowledge and materials coming from the professor. In the United States, students must do research using the library's availability.

In addition, many students do not clearly understand the concept of plagiarism in the United States or Western countries. In some countries, education emphasizes memorization. Furthermore, ideas coming from the professor are considered original. When these seminarians are asked to do research due to a lack of vocabulary to express what they understand, they often take some similar ideas or phrases from other texts without quoting the sources. Consequently, inappropriate authorship and plagiarism are still common mistakes in academic formation programs.

Knowing this, the seminary should thoroughly guide their students and provide clear academic policies to avoid these common errors.

## Affirming One's Identity

Identity crises can make people feel insecure in life. Foreign-born seminarians are often tempted to assimilate into the dominant American culture, which means they often lose their original sense of self. In this way, the concept of a "melting pot" has been disproven in helping immigrants feel at home in America. From the 1970s to the 1980s, the cultural paradigm shifted from the idea of blending cultures together ("melting pot") to celebrating one another's diversity ("salad bowl").

Therefore, the seminary should help reaffirm seminarians' identity when possible. For example, spiritual directors can guide them to appropriately live their faith and devotion practices. Intellectually, professors can assign them homework or research articles related to their own cultures and people. In liturgy, diverse cultures should be celebrated and reflected in the community as a whole.

It is common for many foreign-born seminarians to feel inferior to their native-born peers. By reaffirming their identity, seminaries can help bring them happiness and confidence. With our help, foreign-born priests will gradually grow beyond their "comfort zone" to become familiar with other cultures, in order to serve effectively in future multicultural parish communities.

## Law of the Land

It is very important to help foreign-born seminarians have a basic knowledge of the laws of the United States to avoid unintentional violations. Many gestures or acts are acceptable in their home countries but illegal or unacceptable in the United States. Classes on basic civil law and safe environment practices are essential to not only protecting the seminary, but to protect the priests as well. Often, foreigners violate laws unknowingly, especially on social media platforms, but this does not permit them to escape punishment.

At pastoral placements, such as parishes, hospitals, schools, or prisons, seminarians must be aware of their inappropriate behaviors, as well as misunderstandings caused by their ignorance. Some tend to withdraw or isolate themselves because of safety reasons.

## Relationships with the Diocese

In addition to good relationships with the diocesan brothers, the students should be encouraged to strengthen their relationships with the priests in the diocese. Usually, seminarians have a lot of contact with the vocation director and the bishop during their time in the seminary, but do not know other priests, especially retired priests. When there are opportunities, such as vacations or during the pastoral year, the students should get to know the priests in the diocese to ease their transition into ministry. There are many cases where the day of ordination comes, and the priests do not know who they are, and of course, the students do not know them either.

## Conclusion

The US Church was not fully prepared for the phenomenon of fewer native-born priests serving an increasingly multicultural congregation. Multicultural parishes are a reality, yet the Church is still seeking for more effective solutions to minister to them. We all know that importing foreign-born seminarians to serve the U.S. Church is a temporary solution. What we hope for is fostering priestly vocations from within the United States.

Our goal of forming foreign-born seminarians in the U.S. is not only to solve the problem of fewer native priests, but also to prepare them for more effective and meaningful ministry, and to ensure that they are warmly received in the church. This effort goes beyond addressing immediate challenges—it seeks to build a future in which the Church flourishes in unity in diversity.

As the Church evolves and grows, we must remember to embrace the principle of *"ecclesia semper reformanda."* May we continue striving for ever more effective ways to serve the Church in a rapidly changing world.

> **"Our goal is to prepare foreign-born seminarians for more effective and meaningful ministry, and to ensure that they are warmly received in the Church."**

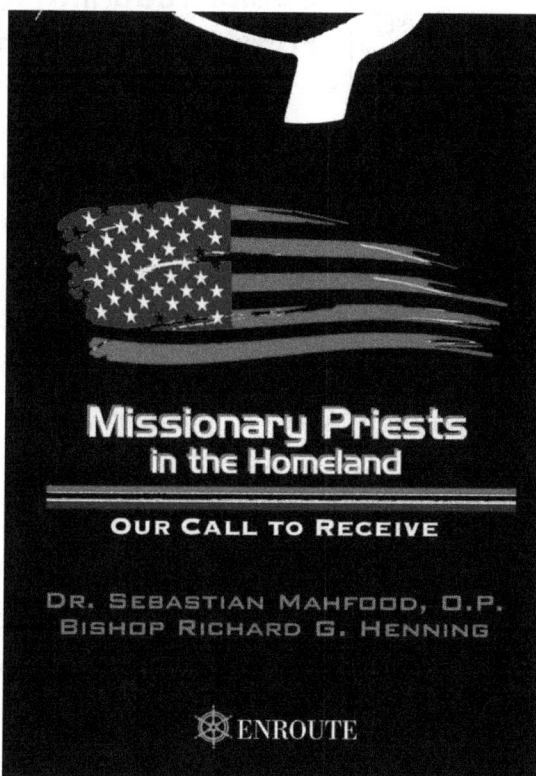

**Missionary Priests in the Homeland**

**OUR CALL TO RECEIVE**

DR. SEBASTIAN MAHFOOD, O.P.
BISHOP RICHARD G. HENNING

ENROUTE

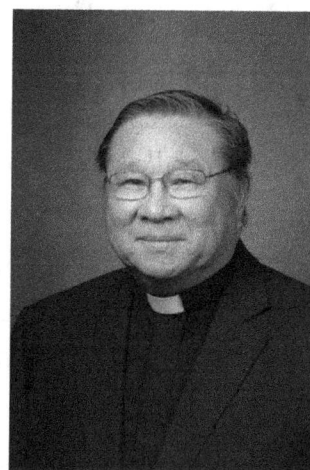

Hy Nguyen, P.S.S., M.A., S.T.D.

Father Hy Nguyen is Associate Professor of Systematic Theology at St. Mary's Seminary & University.

International priests have served the Roman Catholic Church in the United States since its inception. With congregations consisting largely of immigrants or Spanish and French speaking Catholics absorbed by the expansion of US territory, it was only natural that the clergy reflected the remarkable mixture of ethnicities in the Church. New communities lacked the 'home-grown' vocations of more established communities, and the nascent Church needed to recruit or welcome priests and religious from other countries and cultures. It is for these priests and their missionary zeal that this book came to be.

Only 24.95. Available at https://enroutebooksandmedia.com/missionarypriests/

# Political Philosophy and Catholic Social Teaching in Seminary Formation

**John Macias, M.A., S.T.L., Ph.D.**

## Introduction

For many Catholics, the role of philosophy in priestly formation may not be immediately clear. *The Program for Priestly Formation* notes that, "it is essential that seminarians develop an understanding of the relationship between faith and reason and of the relationship and interaction between philosophy and theology, especially the ways they mutually enrich one another."[1] The Church values the contribution philosophy makes both to the work of theology and the formation of her priests. Overall, I see at least three reasons why seminarians study philosophy: (1) preparation for theology, (2) future ministry, and (3) developing awe and wonder at creation. As a seminary professor, I try to ensure that my courses fit one of these categories. I will show how political philosophy can address the first two. Specifically, political philosophy provides the conceptual framework for seminarians to understand and apply Catholic Social Teaching (CST) and to develop the habits of mind for ministry as pastors.

In this essay, I will show how political philosophy, in the tradition of Aristotle and St. Thomas Aquinas, can help us see the continuity within CST and avoid ideological abuse. CST refers to the body of magisterial statements touching on issues involving economics, politics, and overall social life. Political philosophy offers seminarians the interpretive lens needed to grasp the principles of CST in the complex and changing social order of contemporary life. A key component we will see is the concept of a politics of common goods, whether that be the common good of a family, state, or the cosmos. Most today presuppose the beliefs of political liberalism. By liberalism, I do not mean what we generally think of as associated with the Democratic party in the United States. The liberalism I have in mind is the tradition that follows the ideological commitments of figures such as Thomas Hobbes, John Locke, and the American Founders. This meaning of liberalism encompasses both Democrats and Republicans.

> "Political philosophy offers seminarians the interpretive lens needed to grasp the principles of Catholic Social Teaching in a complex and changing social order."

---

[1] Program for Priestly Formation, 6th Edition (Washington, D.C.: United States Conference of Catholic Bishops, 2022), #280.

Given the principles of political liberalism, the use of CST will appear as a series of arbitrary choices to prioritize some values at one time while ignoring them in other contexts. From a Thomistic perspective, however, we can recognize CST as the consistent attempt to apply the principles of the Gospel to a chaotic and changing world. In what follows, I will first describe the ways CST can cause confusion without a proper understanding of its underlying principles. Second, I will describe the rival views of liberal and Thomistic political philosophy and how they address important issues of justice. Finally, I will give a brief description of how a Thomistic view of common goods will allow us to understand the various claims of CST.

## Issues Raised in Catholic Social Teaching

Leo XIII's *Rerum Novarum* often stands as the beginning of CST. Society had shifted from a largely agrarian to industrial order, with working conditions, wages, and conflicts between capitalists and socialists raising important challenges for the Church. *Rerum Novarum* emphasized workers' rights to a living wage and property, and it placed the family as the central starting point of economic life.[2] After this initial document, Pius XI, who called *Rerum Novarum* the *Magna Carta*

of social justice, emphasized the importance of subsidiarity as a way of resisting the totalizing nature of the modern state. As he explains, "it is an injustice and at the same time a grave evil and disturbance of right order to assign to a greater and higher association what lesser and subordinate organizations can do."[3] The state ought to support and aid smaller bodies in the achievement of goods and meeting needs rather than attempt to take their place. These initial works signal that the Church wishes to provide principles that will bring contemporary social life more in line with the Gospel. Both popes identify a place for the state, but they fear the state swallowing up individual and family life.[4] At this point, the language of CST was largely that of classical natural law and focused primarily on justice within individual nations.

In the mid-20th century CST shifted in two ways. First, popes began to employ the language of rights, and second, they expanded the scope of CST from within nations to the entire globe. St. John XXIII contributed significantly to the use of rights language in CST with his *Mater et Magistra* and *Pacem in Terris*. He noted the significant dangers the world faced with the advent of atomic energy, and he emphasized the role of the common good as a point of cooperation between both public and private institutions. Importantly,

[2] Leo XIII, *Rerum Novarum*, in *Catholic Social Thought: Encyclicals and Documents from Pope Leo XIII to Pope Francis*, ed. David J. O'Brien, Thomas A. Shannon (Maryknoll, NY: Orbis Books, 2016), §46. All papal

encyclicals will come from *Catholic Social Thought* unless otherwise noted.
[3] Pius XI, Quadragesimo Anno, §79.
[4] Russell Hittinger, "The Three Necessary Societies," *First Things* June/July 2017, 22.

> **"Without an understanding of its principles, Catholic Social Teaching can appear as a series of arbitrary choices rather than a coherent tradition."**

St. John XXIII first began to use rights as a positive counterpart to the duties of citizens. He offered a long catalogue of rights that citizens ought to possess such as worship, pay, immigration, and civil liberties.[5] The second important transition is the expansion of CST from within one nation to the world as a whole. St. Paul VI, in *Populorum Progressio*, explicitly extends the principles of CST to the global community. St. John Paul II and Benedict XVI spoke to the challenges of globalization in issues of economics and peace, and Pope Francis has made the migration of peoples a major focus of his pontificate, reflected in his 2020 encyclical *Fratelli Tutti*.[6] Francis has called for viewing ourselves as members of a worldwide family when considering questions of the economy along with the dangers facing immigrants. Thus, principles such as human dignity, the universal destination of goods, subsidiarity, and solidarity apply to international relations as well domestically.

These developments, however, raise certain questions of how to prioritize these different principles and rights. What happens when one right conflicts with another? How do we balance one principle with another? Consider the issue of just wages and property. As St. John Paul II describes, a wage is just when it can "suffice for establishing and properly maintaining a family and for providing security for its future."[7] What happens when the need for a business to remain solvent conflicts with what a worker needs to provide for a family? Employers could face the choice of paying workers a living wage but risking closing, or they could remain in operation but fail to pay workers a just wage. Perhaps the state could provide goods for citizens that they fund through taxes, but does this contradict the right to private property? Generally, governments use funds raised through taxation to finance programs aimed at providing food, medical care, or housing to the poor. Some might object that taxation violates the rights of men and women to own their property. Does the right to private property mean that the wealthy have no obligation to the poor? Such a belief would seem to be in strong contrast to the Gospel. Leo XIII asserted a right to own private property, but later popes have qualified this right so that it serves the universal destination of goods.[8] The right to property is not more important than others' right to basic needs. How do we determine when the

---

[5] St. John XXIII, *Pacem in Terris*, §11-27.

[6] St. John Paul II, *Solicitudo Rei Socialis*, §32, Benedict XVI, *Caritas in Veritate*, §53, and Francis, *Fratelli Tutti: On Fraternity and Social Friendship: On Fraternity and Social Friendship* (Huntington, IN: Our Sunday Visitor, 2020), §88-90.

[7] St. John Paul II, *Laborem Exercerns*, §19.

[8] Leo XIII, *Rerum Novarum*, St. Paul VI, *Populorum Progressio*, §23, and St. John Paul II, *Centessimus Annus*, §30-31.

right to private property is subordinate to the needs of others? Furthermore, can we explain these two rights in a way that is not simply contradictory?

International issues present competing claims to rights of nations and peoples. CST clearly identifies a right of men and women to immigrate to other nations to escape violence or out of material need.[9] The Church also affirms the right of nations to regulate who enters their borders and so provide for the safety and security of their citizens.[10] How does a nation balance the work of accepting those seeking refuge from war and poverty with its ability to maintain the material benefits of its citizens and their own cultural identity? Similarly, CST clearly holds that wealthy nations owe poorer nations material resources to meet basic needs and the ability to become self-sufficient.[11] Wealthy nations with massive economies must offer aid to nations struggling to provide food and basic care for their citizens. How much, however, must wealthy nations give to poor nations? Nations may choose to provide medical care or food access to poorer nations while ignoring those within their borders. How do leaders weigh care for their own people against the needs of those in poorer countries? Furthermore, why must the wealthy aid the poor? We recognize the Gospel call to help those in need, but how does one make such an argument to those who do not accept Christianity?

I see at least two reasons why priests, and hence seminarians, must be able to addresses these issues. First, without an answer to these questions, we cannot begin to reverse the trend of CST becoming misused by contemporary political ideologies. By ideology, I mean the sophistical use of arguments and rhetoric for purely partisan ends. We are all too familiar with how CST is often manipulated by political leaders to garner voter support. Certain tenets of CST have become identified with one or other political parties. Catholics often praise the Republican party's traditional position on abortion or family as the reason for their support, while Catholic Democrats emphasize their aid to the poor and immigrants. During campaign season, Catholics will acknowledge the ways in which their own party fails to uphold Catholic teaching, but then they will quickly point out how the rival candidate is far worse. Whether it is abortion or aid to the poor, the failure of their opponents to uphold these teachings serves to excuse the problematic policies of their own party. A major danger for Catholics here is the tendency to identify various aspects of CST with this or that political party. The Catholic Church has no partisan political agenda, but government leaders can use these

---

[9] St. John XXIII, *Mater et Magistra*, §45, St. Paul VI, 67-69§, Benedict XVI, *Caritas in Veritate*, §62, and Francis, *Fratelli Tutti*, §129-131.

[10] *Catechism of the Catholic Church*, §2241, and Francis, *Fratelli Tutti*, §144-145.

[11] St. John XXIII, *Mater et Magistra*, §161-162, and Benedict XVI, *Caritas in Veritate*, §47-48.

various teachings to manipulate votes. The danger is that Catholics begin to see the teachings of the Church as simply one more piece of political propaganda they may accept or ignore.

Secondly, parish priests face the task of guiding their congregations in applying the faith to political activities. In America, men and women find themselves bombarded by a cacophony of voices through news, social media, and pundits telling them they must vote for this or that candidate. Each election is the most important of our lives. Catholics look at candidates for any number of offices and they easily recognize that none is fully compatible with their faith. How then are they to respond? What do they do when faced with the choice between two problematic options? Priests must be able to find ways to present the details of CST that give real guidance but do not fall victim to partisan abuse. Here again with see the danger to the souls of Catholics when they begin to identify various teachings of the Church to rival political parties. Rather than see some principles as liberal or conservative, we need to see how CST is in fact a unified and coherent whole.

In what follows, I will show how the Thomistic political philosophy that underlies CST is opposed to the contemporary political philosophy of liberalism. The rival starting points of liberalism and Thomism mean that they have different ways of answering the questions we have just considered. Liberalism, I will argue, leaves us with the appearance that CST is an arbitrary preference of some values over others, while Thomism allows us to bring these different principles into harmony. Having contrasted their worldviews, I will show how a Thomistic political philosophy presents a coherent narrative for the various political and economic statements found within CST.

> "Thomistic political philosophy views society as the pursuit of a shared common good, not merely individual private benefits."

## Political Philosophy, Rights, and the Common Good

The most important difference between Thomism and liberalism is the way each begins political philosophy. They both try to answer whether society is a shared pursuit for substantive human goods or the coordination of individual pursuits for private benefit. Put differently, is political society more like a symphony orchestra or a public park? For the first view, St. Thomas and Aristotle view society as the pursuit of a shared common good. St. Thomas famously defined law as, "an order of reason for the common good by one who has the care of the community, and promulgated."[12] St. Thomas believes men and women relate to their community as parts to a whole, and law directs them to the flourishing of the

---

[12] St. Thomas Aquinas, *Summa Theologiae*, I-II, q.90, a.4, in *On Law, Morality, and Politics*, trans. Richard J. Regan (Indianapolis, IN: Hackett Publishing Company, 2002).

complete community.[13] On this view, it makes no sense for some individuals to try and gain a greater share of goods or exploit others. The only way we succeed is with others. Indeed, as Charles DeKoninck explains, "the particular does not attain the common good under the note itself of common good if it does not attain it as communicable to others."[14] The common good is a notoriously difficult concept to define, but St. Thomas describes citizens of a political society "as sharing in the final cause, insofar as we call the common good the common end."[15] By final cause, St. Thomas is drawing on the Aristotelian view of teleology, where the final cause is a thing's purpose. Law, on this account, helps citizens understand the way in which their individual choices contribute to their common purpose. As an example, consider a symphony orchestra. All musicians have different roles in an orchestra. Each musician explains why he or she plays these notes at this time by showing how it contributes to their common purpose. The shared final cause, harmonious music, is the purpose and reason for their actions. Musicians playing out of rhythm with the others or trying to gain more attention would detract from the goal of the orchestra. So, if individual musicians try to gain more attention or praise for themselves, they would actually fail to achieve

> **"From a Thomistic view, the common good is the standard of justice rather than individual rights."**

their own good. Musicians can only succeed as musicians in an orchestra by cooperating. In a political society, the choices we all make on a day-to-day basis similarly contribute to the overall flourishing of the community. We can only achieve our individual good by sharing in the success of the whole social order. If we try to take more for ourselves than what is due, we would fail to achieve our own good. Reaching common goods is part of what it means for us to live well as human beings, and we accomplish this good only with our fellow citizens.

On St. Thomas's account, justice is defined by the common good, which determines a community's laws and its citizens' rights. Justice is what citizens owe to one another to reach the common good.[16] If citizens can freely steal from or kill one another, then no shared good is possible. Cooperation requires trust and respect. Therefore, citizens must develop the virtue of justice to achieve the common good. One way of promulgating the requirements of justice is through establishing a set of rights, i.e. legal judgments of what citizens owe each other. Thus, legal rights identify how citizens can act justly. Rights and common goods can also exist outside of individual political communities. Through his metaphysics and account of natural law, St.

---

[13] St Thomas, ST, I-II, q.90, a.2.

[14] Charles De Koninck, "On the Primacy of the Common Good against the Personalists," in *The Writings of Chales De Koninck, Volume* 2, ed. Ralph McInerny (Notre Dame, IN: University of Notre Dame Press, 2009)75.

[15] St. Thomas, *ST*, I-II, q.90, a.2, ad.2. See also Gregory Froelich, "The Equivocal Status of *Bonum Commune*," *The New Scholasticism* 63 (1989): 38-57.

[16] See St. Thomas, *ST*, II-II, q.58, a 5.

Thomas extends common goods and rights to the universe as a whole.[17] God, as the creator and goal of all that exists, is the common good *par excellence*.[18] All creatures find their perfection in God as parts of the whole cosmos. Human beings of different nations might not have the same political common good, but they do share the common good of humanity. Natural law identifies those norms of justice that apply to human beings simply as human beings. Thus, what we call "human rights" refers to the obligations of natural law that we have towards other human beings regardless of their nationality. These rights direct us to the good of the species, the cosmos, and ultimately God.

On the other hand, liberalism does not begin from a shared account of a good human life. The conflicts surrounding the Reformation and Enlightenment led political philosophers to look for ways to secure cooperation that protect against political and religious violence.[19] The answer was to establish a set of rights that allow all citizens to pursue their own view of a good human life. Such agreements make up the well-known concept of the social contract. John Rawls presents a liberal account founded on the classical notion of the social contract.[20] Rawls defends what he calls a "political conception" of justice, which establishes a set of rights independent of any judgments about the objective goods of human life.[21] Rawls's account of justice relies on principles that are political and abstract from metaphysical, ethical, or religious beliefs. Governments then use these political principles of fairness to justify taxes to support social programs, allow practices like abortion or expanding the definition of marriage, and establishing rights to choose one's own way of life. Robert Nozick, although he begins from the same broadly liberal worldview, sharply contrasts Rawls' account. In his work *Anarchy, State, and Utopia*, Nozick takes the same state-of-nature but reaches strongly libertarian conclusions. He presents a notion of the state as a "dominant protective association" that individuals join to seek security from those who treat them unjustly.[22] Nozick uses the imagery of the invisible hand to explain the origin of the state.[23] Individuals do not intend to form a wider community. Rather, through seeking the security of their own individual rights, a minimal state spontaneously arises.[24]

Thomism and liberalism also differ in their understanding of political authority. For Thomists, the purpose of political authority is to secure unity of action for the common good. The Thomist Yves Simon rejects both what he calls

---

[17] Thomas Legge, "Do Thomists Have Rights?" *Nova et Vetera* 17 (2019): 143-144, Angela McKay Knobel, "Aquinas and Rights as Constraints," *The Thomist* 82 (2018): 54.

[18] St. Thomas, *ST*, I-II, q.1, a.8.

[19] Pierre Manent, *An Intellectual History of Liberalism* (Princeton, NJ: Princeton University Press, 1996).

[20] John Rawls, *A Theory of Justice* (Cambridge: Harvard University Press, 1971), 11-12.

[21] John Raws, *Political Liberalism* (New York, NY: Columbia University Press, 2005), 11.

[22] Robert Nozick, *Anarchy, State, and Utopia* (New York, NY: Basic Books, 1974), 113-118.

[23] Nozick, *Anarchy*, 118.

[24] Nozick, *Anarchy*, 120.

the coach-driver theory as well as divine right.[25] By coach-driver, Simon means the belief that political leaders are merely functionaries whose role is to facilitate the wishes of the people, whereas divine right refers to the view that God directly designates individuals to hold ruling power. The essence of authority, Simon argues, is "unifying common action through rule of all."[26] All citizens must be able to pursue the common good, but even amongst virtuous people we cannot guarantee unanimous agreement on how best to achieve that good. Authority allows for a community to begin acting towards its shared goal in the absence of unanimous agreement. The process of designating the person or group who holds the right to possess authority may vary, and the usual means within democratic societies is through voting. In such a case, authority is transferred from the people to elected officials.[27] Representatives then have the responsibility of determining, through their own constitutional means, how the community and its members will reach their common goods.

On this Thomist account, why should citizens obey their government's laws? In many respects, this question harkens back to the relation between the individual and the community. For individuals to reach their own perfection, they must be a part of a community. "Human communities," Simon argues, "are the highest attainments of nature, for they are virtually unlimited with regard to diversity of perfections, and virtually immortal."[28] We achieve greater goods with others than we achieve on our own. Thus, citizens obey the laws and dictates of their leaders because they wish to achieve greater goods. The reason football players follow the plays called by their coaches is because they want to win. A similar relation holds in the obligation of citizens to their leaders. If they wish to achieve the common good of their community, they must follow its laws. The fact that this obligation is conditional is by no mean to suggest that we may easily neglect it. Everyone does in fact desire the common good since we all want to live well. The conditional nature of the obligation explains the reason why citizens have good reasons to follow the laws of their community.

Liberalism cannot rely on any substantive account of justice to require some to obey others. Liberals such as Rawls and Nozick reject a perfectionist understanding of law. Perfectionism is the view that law "should not be neutral about worthwhile forms of life, nor should it exclude moral ideals,

> "Liberalism offers no way to rationally rank conflicting rights, whereas Thomism orders them according to the demands of the common good."

---

[25] Yves Simon, *Philosophy of Democratic Government* (Notre Dame, IN: University of Notre Dame Press, 1993), 146-157.

[26] Yves R. Simon, *A General Theory of Authority* (Notre Dame, IN: University of Notre Dame Press, 1980), 48.

[27] Simon, *Democratic Government*, 76.

[28] Simon, *General Theory*, 29.

or considerations about the good from deliberation about legislation or constitutional essentials."[29] Perfectionists see law as a moral teacher. Lawmakers may outlaw something simply because it is morally evil. On the other hand, Anti-perfectionists like Rawls and Nozick reject the belief that laws can consider anything that is purely moral.[30] In its place, anti-perfectionists argue that law may only prohibit those acts that cause harm to others. To be sure, harm is a somewhat elusive term and often the prevention of one kind of harm requires inflicting another sort. The point, however, is that liberal anti-perfectionists deny that laws may forbid actions purely for their moral quality. For example, should a state outlaw the distribution and use of pornography? We might argue that pornography often involves sexual exploitation when produced, or we could discover that widespread pornography use leads to greater sexual abuse and other violent behaviors. Anti-perfectionists could support criminalizing immoral actions, so long as they also involve harming others. According to anti-perfectionists, we cannot "legislate morality."

Why then, on a liberal account, would citizens obey the law and support the common good? Ultimately, liberalism sees obedience to law as an exchange. It is indeed a social contract. Nozick claims, "there is no moral outweighing of one of our lives by others so as to lead to a greater overall *social* good."[31] We do not sacrifice ourselves to benefit others. Giving over freedoms or material resources requires some benefit in return. For example, following traffic laws means I am limited in the ways I can drive. Abiding by laws establishing the direction of traffic flow means that I do not, in America at least, get to drive on the left side of the road. I give up the freedom to drive 50mph in front of a school by slowing down when I see a 20mph speed limit. When I pay my taxes, I give up the freedom to use that money for other purposes. For a liberal like Nozick, I follow these laws as a matter of contract.[32] We abide by traffic laws so that we can all use roads. If no regulations existed, absolute chaos would ensue and make travel impossible. Paying taxes helps fund police, fire, emergency care, and other public utilities. We do not pay taxes simply for the good of others. If we wanted to help the less fortunate, we would donate to charities. Rawls takes a weaker form of individualism. He agrees that the common good of a community does indeed have a contractual character, but it is not wholly a matter of exchange. He argues that the political community is not a good for individuals "if by such a community we mean a political society united in affirming the same comprehensive doctrine."[33] The community does become a good in itself to the extent that individuals appreciate a society in which all citizens

---

[29] Christopher Tollefsen, "Pure Perfectionism and the Limits of Paternalism," in *Reason, Morality, and Law: The Philosophy of John Finnis*, ed. John Keown and Robert P. George (Oxford: Oxford University Press, 2015), 204.

[30] Rawls, *A Theory of Justice*, 287-290 and Nozick, *Anarchy*, 272-273.

[31] Nozick, 33.

[32] Nozick, 33.

[33] Rawls, *Political Liberalism*, 147.

exercise their rights as they see fit.[34] On Rawls's view, the reason we follow the authority of a political authority is indeed the material benefit we gain, but he also thinks we just ought to desire such a community.

The final difference I wish to consider between Thomism and liberalism concerns the way in which these two theories resolve conflicts between rights. Consider the relation between the right to own property and the right to food, water, and housing. The rights for some to have the basic goods for daily living requires others to give over their property in the form of taxes. Refraining from taxing individuals for the sake of social programs means that some may go hungry. We could also consider the issue of abortion. The right of a woman to determine whether she is pregnant comes up against the child's right to live. From the liberal standpoint, we cannot appeal to a substantive account of human nature and human goods to adjudicate these conflicts. Whether taxation and redistribution are just depends on which right, property or basic goods, is more important. Similarly, the question of abortion means answering if the unborn child is a human being with equal rights or if the right of a child to live imposes burdens on the mother. Resolving these conflicts requires appealing to an account that ranks these various rights. Contemporary society lacks such a shared standard. The

result is that we do not so much resolve these conflicts as end them through judicial fiat. As Alasdair MacIntyre has observed, courts generally serve as the means of reaching negotiated compromises that avoid answering these deeper questions.[35] The upshot is that liberalism lacks a way of rationally demonstrating how we address these conflicts.

Thomists, however, have a definite standard by which to evaluate these scenarios. Ultimately, they all rest on the way in which these different rights relate to the common good in light of the natural law. The issue of property rights compared to the material needs of others clearly relates to the common good. St. Thomas follows Aristotle's distinction between ownership and use,[36] meaning citizens own their property but ought to use it for the fulfillment of the needs of others as well as their own. St. Thomas even argues that, "how the use of private property can be common belongs to the providence of the good lawmaker."[37] State authorities may instruct citizens on how to use their material possessions for the common good. These instructions would likely take the form of taxes that fund various social programs. Since the common good holds priority over individual and private goods, the right to own property is subordinate to the right to use basic goods for life. Regarding abortion, we can easily see how, following natural law, we can

---

[34] Rawls, *Political Liberalism*, 321, and Rawls, *Justice as Fairness*, 291.

[35] Alasdair MacIntyre, *After Virtue: A Study in Moral Theory* (Notre Dame, IN: University of Notre Dame Press, 2007), 253.

[36] St. Thomas, *ST*, II-II, q.66, a.6, and *Commentary*, 97-101.

[37] St. Thomas, *Commentary*, 99.

acknowledge that the right of an unborn child to live outweighs the right to bodily autonomy. Killing innocent people is contrary to the natural law. Thus, permitting such acts would only harm the common good. Therefore, bodily autonomy cannot justify abortion. In both issues, Thomists use the common good and natural law as rational standards to adjudicate conflicts between rights.

## CST with Political Philosophy

Having considered the differences between Thomism and liberalism as political philosophies, I will now show how the Thomistic account of the common good allows us to answer the problems we raised above. Recall, the issues concern conflicts between rights and CST's apparent arbitrary approach. From the perspective of liberalism, we have no clear criteria by which to rank order rights and principles. The liberal state prescinds from any account that would allow us to weigh these objectively, and so we are left with compromising between rights. The result will be a *de facto* ranking of rights. Legislators may offer rhetoric in support of workers or small businesses, but these do not tell us how to respond to issues of workers' pay. In terms of international issues, whether immigration or aid, liberalism presents an even starker and seemingly arbitrary choice between rights. Do we insist on the right of immigrants or nations? The liberal must simply choose whether to prioritize

international or domestic needs. Those who emphasize the rights of immigrants and the poor will advocate for international organizations such as the United States or European Union. Philosophers such as Pierre Manent and Roger Scruton, who prioritize national identities, accuse these international bodies of stripping nations of their cultural identity.[38] No rational way exists for liberals to show whether the right of some nations to their own financial well-being outweighs the needs of poorer nations or vice versa. In such circumstances, CST appears to be a matter of arbitrary preference.

From the Thomistic view, the common good is the standard of justice rather than individual rights. The overall flourishing of the community in accordance with natural law is the source of rights. The common good is served neither by workers living in poverty nor by businesses closing because they cannot afford to pay a just wage. For this reason, the choice is not over which rights to emphasize but rather how to achieve an order in which both workers and business owners can achieve a stable and secure living. As we saw St. Thomas indicate, the state has an obligation to ensure that the use of property be for the common good. The state's use of taxes and social programs provides individuals with the basic needs of life while allowing businesses to remain solvent. The important question, then, is not whose rights take precedence but what does the common good demand.

---

38 Pierre Manent, *A World beyond Politics? A Defense of the Nation-State* (Princeton, NJ: Princeton University Press, 2013), and Roger Scruton, *How to be a Conservative* (London: Bloomsbury Publishing, 2019).

The differences between liberalism and Thomism become even starker when we consider the issues of immigration and international aid. Recall, CST acknowledges both a right to immigrate out of need and the right of nations to monitor and establish norms of entry. Thomism can appeal to the common good that exists between nations and amongst human beings as the means to reconcile the rights of immigrants and nations. Apart from the common good of our individual nation, we also have a common good of the species and all creation.[39] To this extent, the obligation to accept those immigrating out of need is due to the common end of humanity, creation, and God. Such common goods cannot mean the destruction of nations, otherwise it would not actually be a common good. Nor does this principle allow nations to ignore the needs of others simply because they are citizens of another nation. It means all human beings have the same end of God, and therefore our nation is not our sole or highest good. Similarly, the obligation that wealthy nations foster the economies of poorer nations does not follow from a moralistic commitment to altruism. The Thomist can point to the common good of humanity and all nations as the norm to determine both why wealthy nations have an obligation to poorer nations and the way they provide aid. The international common good is not served through some nations permanently subsidizing others. For this reason, we see CST warn against allowing developing countries to become dependents on wealthier states. The common flourishing of humanity is better served when all nations are capable of self-sufficiency and providing for their own citizens.

## Conclusion

The overall purpose of this essay has been to illustrate the kind of political philosophy that best explains the tradition of CST. This Thomist philosophy helps us to apply and defend the principles of CST. We saw above that the primary political philosophy competing with Thomism is liberalism. Whereas Thomism emphasizes the common good and the role of law in establishing virtue, liberalism begins with rights and seeks to find the best way to fulfill as many rights as possible. The role of government is not to guide citizens to a particular understanding of goods. Instead, laws secure the conditions necessary for individuals to live out the view of a good life they particularly hold. As we have seen, a liberal view of politics leads many of the principles of CST to appear arbitrary or even contradictory. It offers no way for us to show how political leaders can rationally rank order goods. The common good of Thomism, however, provides us with a criterion for determining when one right should take priority over others.

---

[39] St. Thomas, *SCG*, II, c.42, 44-45.

For seminarians, the study of political philosophy then is important both for their understanding of CST and their future work as pastors. One of the great temptations for Catholics today is to view their religious faith through the lens of partisan politics. Many of us know the various teachings that become equated with one political party over another. The tendency is for Catholics to modify their religious beliefs to fit their politics rather than changing their politics to fit their religion. Catholics who strongly advocate for the rights of the unborn, the needs of families, and strong religious freedoms sometimes fail to acknowledge the rights to healthcare, education, and immigration. Other Catholics rightly point to the preferential option for the poor and identify Christ in the stranger and outcast, but they seem to downplay the need to protect the unborn and uphold a

> **"Political philosophy gives seminarians the tools to be shepherds and guides to God's people."**

Christian view of family life. In reality, Catholics today are politically homeless. Priests, to be true pastors and shepherds, cannot become just one more voice in the political fray. Rather, they must help their people in learning to see CST as how we build up the kingdom of God on earth. Political philosophy presents seminarians with the important principles underlying CST. Thus, it gives them the tools they need to be shepherds and guides to God's people.

John Macias, M.A. S.T.L., Ph.D.
Doctor Macias is Assistant Professor of Philosophy at St. Mary's Seminary & University.

A relatively complete basis for the understanding of political science as presented by Aristotle, with the help of Saint Thomas Aquinas mainly by way of his (partial) commentary on Aristotle's *Politics* and his own work "On Kingship".

Only $24.95. Available at https://enroutebooksandmedia.com/politicalscienceandsaintthomasaquinas/

# Teaching Catholic History in Seminary Formation

## Dennis Castillo, M.A., Ph.D.

### Why Study History?

For most people, history is a set of facts, a collection of events, a series of things that happened, one after another, in the past. As Peter Stearns, retired professor from George Mason University has explained, history is so much more- it is a way of thinking about and seeing the world.

"To genuinely make sense of the past," he argues, "you need to learn how to see it on its own terms, how to make the strange and unfamiliar logical and comprehensible, and how to empathize with people who once thought so differently than we do today. If you learn how to do these things, you begin to cultivate a crucial set of skills that not only help navigate the past, but the present as well."[1] By gaining experience in making sense of unfamiliar modes of thought and behavior, we are better equipped to understand a modern world inhabited with diverse peoples and ideas. History offers the opportunity to explore different regions, cultures, and a wide variety of human experiences.

"It might seem counterintuitive," Stearns continues, "that one of the best ways to illuminate the present is by studying the past, but that is precisely why history can be so important. When we appreciate that history is

> "History is not, first and foremost, a body of knowledge, but rather a way of thinking."

not, first and foremost, a body of knowledge, but rather a way of thinking, it becomes a particularly powerful tool."[2] Through the study of history, a person develops critical, interpretive thinking skills through in-depth analysis of primary and secondary source materials; the ability to identify different types of sources of historical knowledge; and analytical writing skills and close reading skills.

### Catholic History

While the study of history is a vital part of any student's education, Catholic history actually encompasses a variety of historical fields. It is intellectual history, studying theological developments and doctrinal controversies. It is political history, including such topics as the fall of the Roman Empire, the Papal States, and the unification of Italy. Art history is prominent, with the

---

[1] "Why Study History? Revisited," Peter N. Stearns. *Perspectives in History*, September 18, 2020.

https://www.historians.org/perspectives-article/why-study-history-revisited-september-2020/

[2] Ibid.

Church's use of religious art to catechize the faithful, as well as recording great artistic developments, such as the Romanesque and Gothic styles of architecture. It can include liturgical history, tracing developments in worship. American Catholic history requires an understanding of the sociological impact of immigration on an evolving Catholic community, as well as the Nativist reaction to these developments. It is even economic history, helping students to understand the impact of the Industrial Revolution in order to appreciate Leo XIII's 1891 response to it in *Rerum Novarum*.

## Teaching Catholic History

Catholic history is a subject found in a variety of educational institutions and departments. It is taught in both private and public educational institutions and can be situated in History, Humanities, Religious Studies, Theology, or Catholic Studies departments.

I have taught Catholic history at the undergraduate and graduate level for the past thirty-eight years in small Catholic liberal arts colleges, large Catholic universities, public universities, and seminaries. Outside of the seminary world, these courses could fulfill history or religious studies degree requirements. More often, they help non-majors to satisfy general education requirements or serve as electives. When teaching at Catholic educational institutions, it is important to be mindful of the specific charism and heritage of the religious order that founded the school. In this way, Catholic history makes an important contribution to understanding the mission and values of the insti-

> "Catholic history actually encompasses a variety of historical fields—intellectual, political, liturgical, and artistic."

tution. I have experienced this at schools founded by Jesuits, Vincentians, Franciscans, and Religious Sisters of Mercy. While teaching at these institutions has been very rewarding, the most meaningful experience has been teaching Catholic history as a core subject to those preparing for careers in pastoral ministry.

## Catholic history in pastoral ministry programs

Those preparing for ministry in the Catholic Church find themselves in a community steeped in history. The clergy's alb is derived from first century attire. The division of the Late Roman Empire into dioceses continues today in Catholic ecclesiastical organization. And bishops are powerful pieces on a chess board for good reason.

Catholic history is an integral part of programs preparing individuals for careers in pastoral ministry. Since students are preparing for definite ministries in the Catholic Church, there is a greater emphasis on the history of Catholicism as an institution.

There are ecclesial documents guiding the formation of lay people, permanent deacons, and seminarians. For Catholic lay students, this is *Co-Workers in the Vineyard of the Lord: A Resource for Guiding the Development of Lay Ecclesial Ministry*. This states: "Intellectual formation should be as broad and deep as possible, with exposure to the vast range of topics and subjects that constitute Catholic theology." Church history is cited as a discipline to be included, but it does not go into any further detail about content.[3]

> "Those preparing for ministry in the Catholic Church find themselves in a community steeped in history."

In 2023 there were 164 lay ecclesial ministry formation programs sponsored or co-sponsored by the local diocese, an increase of 11% from 2010.[4] Most lay ecclesial ministry programs grant certificates of completion and are taught at the undergraduate level. A typical church history course in such a program would teach everything from the Early Church to American Catholic history in 20 contact hours.[5]

The most popular graduate degrees for lay ministers are the Master of Arts in Pastoral Ministry and the Master of Arts in Theology. Unfortunately, these programs generally require only three credits in church history. Unless there is a class covering the whole of church history, students often need to choose between a course focusing just on ancient and medieval church history or another course limited to Reformation and modern church history. The exception would be MDiv degrees designed for lay people that usually require six credits of church history.

Formation for permanent deacons is guided by the *National Directory for the Formation, Ministry, and Life of Permanent Deacons in the United States*. Modeled after the Program for Priestly Formation (PPF), it speaks of Four Dimensions of Formation: Intellectual, Pastoral, Spiritual, and Human.

In Intellectual Formation, the Directory emphasizes Sacred Scripture ("the soul of the program"), liturgical studies, and preaching. Two other areas of emphasis that would involve church history are the study of Catholic social encyclicals, addressing "immigration as experienced within the Church in America," and interfaith and ecumenical study, to understand "the beliefs and practices of other religions and Christian denominations."[6] As far as church history itself in the formation of permanent deacons, it should be an introduction to the Fathers, "and an elementary knowledge of the history of the

---

[3] *Co-Workers in the Vineyard of the Lord: A Resource for Guiding the Development of Lay Ecclesial Ministry* (Washington, DC: USCCB, 2005), 45-46.

[4] "Catholic Ministry Formation Enrollments: Statistical Overview for 2009-2010," CARA, 27.

[5] "U.S. Lay Ecclesial Ministry Formation Programs," The CARA Report, Fall 2023, 9.

[6] *National Directory for the Formation, Ministry, and Life of Permanent Deacons in the United States* (USCCB, 2005), #119.

Church,"[7] that is, a broad survey course with an emphasis on Patristics.

There were 140 programs in 2022-23 for deacon candidates. On average, these programs required five years of training to complete and could be at either the undergraduate or graduate level.[8] The Diocese of Buffalo went from an undergraduate certificate program, with a 20 hour church history class, to a graduate degree with 45 contact hours in church history. Some programs, however, do not teach church history. At St. Bernard's Institute in Rochester, for example, any elective in historical theology fulfills the church history requirement.

## Catholic History in Seminary Formation

Church history is more prominent in the curriculum of the formation of future priests. The 1884 Third Plenary Council of Baltimore lengthened the course of studies for major and minor seminaries to six years for each program.[9] The minor seminary program was to follow a six-year classical program, which included courses in Christian doctrine, Latin, English, mathematics, geography, and penmanship. History was included in this curriculum, but it was of a general education nature and not specifically church history.

The six-year major seminary curriculum was divided into two years of philosophy, followed by four years of theology. The philosophy program included courses on the history of philosophy. Church history (*Historia Ecclesiastica*) was taught three hours a week in the first two years of the theology program, which represented 8% of instruction hours. The theology program placed a heavy emphasis on dogmatic and moral theology, with over half of the curriculum (54%) devoted to these two subjects.[10]

The Catholic Master of Divinity is a substantial professional degree. While the Master of Divinity can be earned with as few as 72 credit hours in other denominations, in the Catholic Church the MDiv requires approximately 120 credit hours. A major development in American seminary education after Vatican II was seeking academic accreditation for MDiv programs. In the early 1970s seminaries became members of the Association of Theological Schools, as well as various regional accreditors such as the North Central Association or the Middle States Commission on Higher Education.

## Governing Documents - Secular

Most Catholic seminaries are dual accredited- belonging to a regional accreditor, as well as the Association of Theological Schools (ATS)

---

[7] *National Directory for the Formation, Ministry, and Life of Permanent Deacons in the United States* (Washington, DC: USCCB, 2005), #124.

[8] "U.S. Diaconate Formation Programs," The CARA Report, Fall 2023, 9.

[9] Joseph White, *The Diocesan Seminary in the United States: A History from the 1780s to the Present* (Notre Dame, IN: University of Notre Dame Press, 1989), 161.

[10] Ibid., 237-39.

which accredits schools of various denominations. Both ATS and the regional associations are secular bodies approved by the United States Department of Education for accreditation purposes.

Regional accreditors, such as the Middle States Commission on Higher Education (MSCHE) are not concerned with the religious objectives of the MDiv, but only whether it conforms to accepted educational practices. For MSCHE, this is determined in Standard III: Design and Delivery of the Student Learning Experience: "An institution provides students with learning experiences that are characterized by rigor and coherence…All learning experiences…are consistent with higher education expectations."[11]

A major accreditation concern is educational assessment. For MSCHE, this is found in Standard V: Educational Effectiveness Assessment. Schools are to have "clearly stated student learning outcomes at the institution and degree/program levels, which are interrelated with one another, with relevant educational experiences, and with the institution's mission." Faculty are to regularly conduct "organized and systematic assessments…evaluating the extent of student achievement of institutional and degree/program goals."[12] Professors of church history need to be able to articulate how their courses contribute to the learning objectives of the MDiv, as well as

document success and areas needing improvement.

Of the two secular accreditors, ATS is more useful for seminaries. ATS addresses MDiv programs in Standard 4. Similar to the PPF, Standard 4 states that the MDiv should be "broadly and deeply attentive to the intellectual, human, spiritual, and vocational dimensions of student learning and formation." Church history primarily contributes to Standard 4 in the area of religious heritage, which includes "the theological traditions and history of the school's faith community, and the broader heritage of other relevant religious traditions."[13] Church history also contributes in the area of cultural context by attending to "cultural and social issues, to global awareness and engagement, and to the multifaith and multicultural nature of the societies in which students may serve."[14]

## Governing Documents - Catholic

The Holy See has a long history of concern for theological education. In 1931, Pope Pius XI issued the apostolic constitution *Deus Scientiarum Dominus*, which laid down a new system of Rules for Universities and Faculties of Ecclesiastical Studies. It was the first time that the Church had promulgated a plan of studies that would be common to all ecclesiastical faculties throughout the whole world. In article 7 it

[11] www.msche.org/standards/fourteenth-edition/#standard3.

[12] www.msche.org/standards/fourteenth-edition/#standard5.

[13] www.ats.edu/files/galleries/standards-of-accreditation, 4.3.a.

[14] www.ats.edu/files/galleries/standards-of-accreditation, 4.3.b.

specified the academic degrees to be offered by ecclesiastical faculties: Baccalaureate, Licentiate, and Doctorate.[15] *Deus Scientiarum Dominus* specified that the main subjects for the S.T.B. include Ecclesiastical History, Patrology, and Christian Archaeology. It did not, however, indicate the amount of instruction to be dedicated to any of the required disciplines.[16]

The next major document regarding theological education was Vatican II's *Optatam Totius* issued in 1965. It was intended that this document would be adapted by episcopal conferences to establish a local "program of priestly training."[17]

In the revision of ecclesiastical studies, greater emphasis was placed on scripture and patristics, with the latter assigned to professors of dogmatic theology. In addition to studying the contribution of the Fathers of the Eastern and Western Church, the "further history of dogma should also be presented, account being taken of its relation to the general history of the Church."[18] This is one of the many areas where church history professors should coordinate with their colleagues.

In article 16, church history was presented as necessary for assisting theology, so that the "theological disciplines be renewed through a more living contact with the mystery of Christ and the history of salvation." The Council's emphasis on ecumenism and inter-faith dialogue also opened new opportunities for church history. Seminarians were to "be brought to a fuller understanding of the churches and ecclesial communities separated from the Apostolic Roman See...Let them also be introduced to a knowledge of other religions which are more widespread in individual regions, so that they may acknowledge more correctly what truth and goodness these religions, in God's providence, possess, and so that they may learn to refute their errors..."[19] Church history courses would need to include more on the conflicts between religious communities, the issues involved, and the efforts to heal divisions.

After the Council, the first American PPF was issued by the National Conference of Catholic Bishops on January 18, 1971. It was recognized that, influenced as it was by the European system of education, Vatican II affirmed the necessity of major seminaries with a six-year formation period. The American equivalent to the conciliar "major" or six-year seminary would be the final two years of college and four years of professional theological study.[20]

---

[15] www.vatican.va/content/pius-xi/la/apost_constitutions/documents/hf_p-xi_apc_19310524_deus-scientiarum-dominus.html, no. 7.

[16] Ibid., #27.

[17] www.vatican.va/archive/hist_councils/ii_vatican_council/documents/vat-ii_decree_19651028_optatam-totius_en.html, no.1.

[18] Ibid., no. 16.

[19] Ibid.

[20] *The Program of Priestly Formation of the National Council of Bishops* (Washington, D.C.: NCCB, 1971), no. 10.

In the revision of the curriculum, the 1971 PPF stressed that key elements of theological formation be kept in balance, "study of the Bible as the inspired expression of divine revelation, historical study of the theological developments in the past, and a sound treatment of fundamental doctrines through systematic theology."[21]

This contribution of history was described in Chapter Two in the section titled "The Historical Dimension of Theological Study." This encouraged a greater awareness of the historical dimension of every subject in the curriculum: "All courses must help the student develop a critical sense of history and an insight into the richness as well as the limitations of the varying cultural expressions of the Christian faith through the centuries." While students often regard the past as irrelevant, they need to see "that present problems cannot be understood without a knowledge of the past. To accomplish, he must understand the critical methodology of history."[22]

Two extremes were to be avoided in presenting this historical dimension. The first was presenting the Church as immutable, with no sense of doctrinal development, or promoting one period of Church history as the model for others. The other extreme would be "an excessive relativism which would destroy continuity with the past and which would lose sight of the fact that Christianity is above all an historical religion."[23]

Regarding the teaching of church history, the 1971 PPF devoted three articles to the discipline.

Article 56 emphasized that students should appreciate the life of the Church and the development of her teaching. Seminarians were to be introduced to historical methodology and

> **"Seminarians must develop a critical sense of history and an insight into the richness and limitations of cultural expressions of faith."**

taught to seek the facts, avoiding a romanticized view of the past or an undue stress on apologetics. At the same time, the teaching of history needed to be more than merely factual, it should contribute to developing "a theological insight into the mission of the Church and the significances of her historic experiences for her life today. Historical studies should be closely integrated into all the student's theological work, so that he acquires an appreciation of the historical aspect of theological problems."[24]

Article 57 addresses content. In addition to a general course of church history, electives should be provided in the following periods: early church history and patrology, particularly in view of the Council's stress on return to the sources; the medieval period, with emphasis on the influence of scholasticism in the creative development of theology; the Reformation period, in view of its importance to ecumenism; and the modern period, studying the impact of the growth of science and of critical historical

---

[21] Ibid., no. 28.
[22] Ibid., no. 29.
[23] Ibid., no. 30.
[24] Ibid., no. 56.

methodology on humanity's understanding of itself and the world. There should also be a course on the history of the Church in the United States, with an emphasis on the diversity present in the Church in America due to immigration.[25] The study of the history of the development of dogma is stressed by article 58, but this could either be an elective or part of the regular courses in systematic theology.[26]

In addition to ecumenism, the 1971 PPF also called for seminarians being introduced "to a knowledge of the non-Chrisitan religions represented in" their region.[27] Here was another area for church history to contribute. Like the Council, the PPF stressed that special attention should be given to Judaism. Church history courses should include "the heritage Christians have received from the Jews," as well as am understanding of "the often tragic Jewish-Christian relations[28] Seminary faculty were "expected to demonstrate an ecumenical awareness in attitude and teaching, and a sympathetic respect for other traditions."[29] When teaching about other religious traditions, the faculty were to encourage seminarians "to view these traditions as their own adherents understand them, rather than in a negative or polemical manner."[30]

The 1990 Synod of Bishops addressed priestly formation. In 1992 Pope John Paul II followed up by issuing the post-synodal apostolic exhortation

*Pastores Dabo Vobis (I Will Give You Shepherds)*: "On the Formation of Priests in Circumstances of the Present Day." Its most significant contribution to priestly formation, including church history, was its emphasis on human formation.

Human formation was presented as the basis of all priestly formation: "The whole work of priestly formation would be deprived of its necessary foundation if it lacked a suitable human formation."[31] While the ministry of the priest is to proclaim the word, celebrate the sacraments, and guide the Christian community, this is always done in collaboration with human beings. To succeed in his ministry, the priest "should mold his human personality in such a way that it becomes a bridge and not an obstacle for others in their meeting with Jesus Christ the Redeemer of humanity…the priest should be able to know the depths of the human heart, to perceive difficulties and problems, to make meeting and dialogue easy, to create trust and cooperation, to express serene and objective judgments."[32]

Future priests needed to cultivate those human qualities needed for them to be balanced people, strong and free, capable of handling the stresses of pastoral responsibilities. *Pastores Dabo Vobis* emphasized in particular the ability to relate to others: "This is truly fundamental for a person who is called to be responsible for a community and to be a "man of communion."

[25] Ibid., no. 57.
[26] Ibid., no. 58.
[27] Ibid., no. 257.
[28] Ibid., no. 258.
[29] Ibid., no. 269.

[30] Ibid., no. 270.
[31] www.vatican.va/content/john-paul-ii/en/apost_exhortations/documents/hf_jp-ii_exh_25031992_pastores-dabo-vobis.html, no. 48.
[32] Ibid.

This demands that the priest not be arrogant, or quarrelsome, but affable, hospitable, sincere in his words and heart, prudent and discreet, generous and ready to serve, capable of opening himself to clear and brotherly relationships and of encouraging the same in others, and quick to understand, forgive and console."[33] In the study of history, students can see actual cases demonstrating how a person's personality impacted their relationships with others and the consequences. It can help them become more aware of what gifts they bring to ministry and what challenges to overcome.

The 4th edition of the PPF came out shortly after *Pastores Dabo Vobis* in 1992. Even though it stated that this edition, in its final stages, was "enriched at every point" by the apostolic exhortation and called it "a charter document for priestly formation worldwide," human formation was not included. The focus remained limited to spiritual, intellectual, and pastoral formation.[34]

The 4th edition laid out the format of church history courses that has remained to this day, stating that "the core should include Patristics, Early, Medieval, Modern, and Contemporary Church History; and American Church History. American Church History should be taught in a way that reflects the multicultural origins of the Church in the United States. Among historical studies, the study of patristics is of special

importance." This has resulted in a fairly common three course section of Church History-I (Ancient and Medieval, with a stress on Patristics), Church History-II (Reformation and Modern), and American Church History.[35] The 4th edition also stated that, to preach effectively, seminarians needed to "understand the world in which the message of Christ is preached" and so a knowledge of history was invaluable.[36]

In 2006, the 5th edition of the PPF achieved the full implementation of *Pastores dabo vobis* with its focus on the four dimensions of formation: human, spiritual, intellectual, and pastoral. Human formation and church history will be addressed more fully below.

More stress was placed on the Fathers: "Patristic studies constitute an essential part of theological studies. Theology should draw from the works of the Fathers of the Church that have lasting value within the living tradition of the Church." Church history was to provide patrology (an overview of the life and writings of the Fathers) and Systematics focus on patristics proper (the theology of the Fathers).[37]

The 2006 PPF repeated what had been said regarding historical studies in 1992, but added: "Among historical studies, the study of patristics and the lives of the saints are of special importance."[38] While promoting role models in

---

[33] Ibid.

[34] *The Program of Priestly Formation of the National Council of Bishops,* 4th edition (Washington, D.C.: NCCB, 1992), iii.

[35] Ibid., no. 372.

[36] Ibid., no. 344.

[37] *The Program of Priestly Formation of the United States Conference of Catholic Bishops,* 5th edition (Washington, D.C.: USCCB, 2006), no. 201.

[38] Ibid., no. 210.

church history is necessary, it is important to avoid drifting into hagiography.

In 2016 a new *Ratio Fundamentalis Institutionis Sacerdotalis* was issued, titled "The Gift of the Priestly Vocation." It divided priestly formation into four stages: the 'propaedeutic stage', the 'stage of philosophical studies' or 'discipleship stage', the 'stage of theological studies' or 'configuration stage', and the 'pastoral stage' or 'stage of vocational synthesis'. The MDiv program takes place within the configuration stage.[39]

A great emphasis is on integrating the dimensions of formation: "The concept of integral formation is of the greatest importance, since it is the whole person, with all that he is and all that he possesses who will be at the Lord's service in the Christian community."[40] The theological disciplines, likewise, must be integrated. Church history cannot be isolated from other areas of study. It needs to be part of a "unified, integral journey, in which each subject is an important 'tile in the mosaic' for presenting the mystery of Christ and the Church."[41]

One area of this intellectual integration is the collaboration between church history and dogmatic theology in understanding the contributions of the Fathers of the Church, from both East and West.[42] Another area of collaboration is in teaching the social doctrine of the Church, which requires "a deep knowledge of reality and a reading of human, social and political relations."[43]

Finally, regarding the field of church history itself, the *Ratio* emphasizes the scientific examination of historical sources to document the origin and development of the Church as the People of God. This development did not take place in a vacuum, so in relating the history of the Church, "the concrete social, economic and political situations should be taken into account, as should the opinions and categories of thought that have exerted most influence, without neglecting to investigate their reciprocal interdependence and development."[44]

A year after the *Ratio* a new apostolic constitution on ecclesiastical universities and faculties was issued by Pope Francis, *Veritatis Gaudium*, which went into effect January 29, 2018. One area of significance for church history was its emphasis that Christianity does not have only one cultural expression. It is important to "reflect the different faces of the cultures and peoples in which it is received and takes root'."[45] We can see this diversity in the early Christian community, as the original Jewish Christians succeeded in converting Gentiles from the Greek and Latin cultures. In fact, before the destruction of Jerusalem in 70, one could describe Christianity as a tri-cultural religion- Jewish, Greek, and Latin.

---

[39] www.clerus.va/content/dam/clerus/documenti/ratio-2026/Ratio-EN-2017-01-03, no. 57.

[40] Ibid, no. 92.

[41] Ibid, no. 153.

[42] Ibid, no. 168.

[43] Ibid., no. 172.

[44] Ibid., no. 173.

[45] www.vatican.va/content/francesco/en/apost_constitutions/documents/papa-francesco_costituzione-ap_20171208_veritatis-gaudium.html, no. 4.

The 6th and most recent edition of the PPF went into effect on August 4, 2023, the Feast of St. John Vianney. Its central operating theme is that priestly formation is integrated, grounded in community and missionary in spirit.[46] It is integrated in that the four dimensions of human, spiritual, intellectual, and pastoral formation are woven together, while still remaining distinct.[47] It is communitarian in that the call to priesthood is more than an individual response. It takes place within the family, parish, and wider Christian community.[48] Finally, future priests are called to the same missionary discipleship that is expected of all members of the People of God.[49]

The new PPF lists a series of challenges facing formation today: "Priestly formation takes place in a given ecclesial and historical context. Identifying that context is a critical task for giving shape to particular programs of formation."[50] This context includes secularism, social injustice, violence, relativism, immigration, religious discrimination, and the role of women. Each of these challenges can and should be addressed in church history in collaboration with the other theological disciplines, as well as the other dimensions of formation.[51]

Regarding specific coursework, the 6th edition repeats what was said regarding Patristics and Church History in the previous edition of the PPF. A new area within intellectual formation was the need to increase awareness of ecology: "Seminarians must be familiar with Church teaching on the subject and be encouraged to experience an ecological conversion."[52] While understanding the Industrial Revolution is important to appreciating Leo XIII's teachings in *Rerum Novarum*, the ecological impact of heavy industry should also be included.

> "Church history helps us to see the real Church and to love her as she truly exists, learning from both her successes and failures."

The most recent guidance on the teaching of church history was a letter by Pope Francis issued on November 21, 2024. The study of church history is important "in order to help priests better interpret the world in which we live."[53] Francis asserted that church history plays a valuable role in protecting the study of theology from "ecclesiological monophysitism," which he defined as "an overly angelic conception of the Church, presenting a Church that is unreal because she lacks spots and wrinkles...Church history helps us to see the real Church and to love the Church as she

---

[46] *The Program of Priestly Formation of the United States Conference of Catholic Bishops,* 6th edition (Washington, D.C.: USCCB, 2022), no. 4.

[47] Ibid., no. 11.

[48] Ibid., no. 13.

[49] Ibid., no. 14.

[50] Ibid, no. 17.

[51] Ibid., nos. 18-21.

[52] Ibid., no. 336.

[53] "Letter of His Holiness Pope Francis on the Renewal of the Study of Church History," www.vatican.va/content/francesco/en/letters/2024/documents/20241121-letters-storia-chiesa.html

truly exists, and love what she has learnt and continues to learn from her mistakes and failures."[54]

Francis quoted from his 2020 encyclical *Fratelli Tutti* (On Fraternity and Social Friendship) to say that church history must see to it that the sins of the past not be forgotten: "Nowadays, it is easy to be tempted to turn the page, to say that all these things happened long ago and we should look to the future. For God's sake, no! We can never more forward without remembering the past: we do not progress without an honest and unclouded memory...I think not only of the need to remember the atrocities, but also all those who, amid such great inhumanity and corruption, retained their dignity and, with gestures small and large, chose the part of solidarity, forgiveness and fraternity. To remember goodness is also a healthy thing. Forgiving does not mean forgetting...In the face of something that cannot be forgotten for any reason, we can still forgive."[55]

Finally, on the teaching of church history, Francis made the observation that church history needs a more equal footing in theological education. Too often church history is reduced to "secondary topic within theology, resulting in a form of theology that ultimately shows itself incapable of truly entering into dialogue with the profound and existential reality of the man and woman of our time."[56]

## Church History and the contemporary MDiv

Regarding nomenclature, in a review of ten Catholic seminaries, the term "Historical Studies" was used by two schools. The rest used the term "Church History." In eight of these seminaries, these programs were located in distinct church history departments, while in the other two church history was in the department of systematic theology. Finally, in these same ten Catholic seminaries, the average number of credit hours required in Church History for the Master of Divinity degree was 9.6.

In the typical Catholic MDiv program there are generally three church history courses: Ancient and Medieval, Reformation and Modern, and American Catholicism. Patristics is sometimes taught as a separate course, which is located in either the history or systematic theology departments. In the typical seminary, with just one historian on the faculty, professors often need to be generalists.

In the typical three course sequence of church history, there are a variety of issues raised which are important for future ministers of the Church. In the Ancient and Medieval course, there is an important lesson in the very breadth it covers. We begin in the ancient world, where Christianity is counter-cultural, being persecuted by the state. In the second half of the course, medieval Christianity dominates European culture. We see

---

[54] Ibid.

[55] Ibid.

[56] Ibid.

that Christianity has survived, and thrived, in a variety of settings, that there is no one single ideal relationship of church and state. Another issue which covers both halves of the course is the papacy. We begin with the early bishops of Rome and end with the powerful medieval pontificates. Where can we see papal primacy present with Peter and his early successors? How does this papal primacy develop as we head into the late medieval and modern eras? There is also the issue of religion and violence. There are no heresy trials in the early Church, even though fundamental issues such as the Trinity and Christology, are being hotly contested. This is followed by the crusading movement and other episodes of violence. When does this violent element originate in Christianity and what are the causes?

Issues in the Reformation and Modern course include questions such as: What reform movements were present in the Church before Luther? What were the causes of the Reformation and the issues involved? What is the status of the modern ecumenical movement in addressing these issues? Were the Wars of Religion really about religion? What has been the Church's relationship with modern world? What are the challenges to bringing the Gospel to the world of today?

Regarding the course on American Catholic history, in half of Catholic seminaries it is called "American Catholicism," while the other half use the term "United States Church History."

Important issues in American Catholic historiography include questions such as: Can we speak of an American-Catholic community in the same way as we speak of Irish, Italian, Polish, or French Catholicism? What is an American-Catholic? How has immigration effected American Catholicism? What is the legacy of immigration today? Nativists claimed that Catholicism and democracy were incompatible. How has the Church contributed to American society? Finally, this course can play a key role in the inculturation of the increasing number of international seminarians today.

## Catholic History and Formation

In the current PPF, intellectual formation includes providing seminarians with competence in philosophy. One advantage in teaching seminarians, compared to lay and deacon candidates, is the solid foundation received in philosophy. This is helpful in teaching church history. When addressing the complex theological controversies in the Early Church, as well as the theology of Medieval Christianity, church history professors can expect a degree of familiarity with Greek philosophy, particularly Plato and Aristotle.[57]

> **"The theological disciplines must form a unified, integral journey, not isolated fields of study."**

---

[57] www.clerus.va/content/dam/clerus/documenti/ratio-2026/Ratio-EN-2017-01-03, no. 116.

The theological disciplines cannot be isolated fields of study, but must be integrated. At St. Mary's Seminary and University church history is located in the department of systematic and liturgical theology. This has led to fruitful department meetings where colleagues discuss areas of overlap and how to better support one another. Such collaboration is necessary to achieve that "unified, integral journey" which the 2016 *Ratio* called for in intellectual formation.[58] While church history is part of intellectual formation, it also contributes to the other dimensions as well.

Human formation, described as "the foundation of all priestly formation," promotes the integral growth of the seminarian as a person. Its goal is that the seminarian "will become a responsible person able to make the right decisions, gifted with right judgement and able to have an objective perception of persons and events." In church history, seminarians are presented with a variety of examples of Christian leadership. Studying the actions of these church leaders, and the consequences, can assist seminarians in valuing human formation. They can see the importance of addressing harmful behaviors, as well as discerning their own talents and how to best place them at the service of the People of God. Examples of such great leaders would be John Carroll and James Gibbons, both men who possessed the social graces which helped make possible their success in representing the Catholic faith to the wider American public.[59]

In spiritual formation, knowledge of and meditation on the Fathers of the Church is to be promoted, "since they are witnesses to the life of the People of God over two thousand years." Church history contributes to the spiritual dimension by examining the lives of these great men. While the writings of these individuals is central to the development of Catholic theology, the story of their lives also contributes to spiritual formation. The fact that many died for the faith as martyrs gives them a special place in the Church. Justin Martyr's attempt to reconcile Greek philosophy with the Gospel in his appeal to his former pagan colleagues is an example of the 2016 *Ratio*'s view that the Father's work "led to the emergence of an 'explosive vitality', missionary fervor and an atmosphere of love that inspired souls to heroism in daily life"[60]

Furthermore, church history contributes to spiritual formation by studying the origin and development of the liturgical year, the variety of the charisms among the many religious orders, and the development of Christian worship. Students come to understand the rich history of the Catholic spiritual tradition.

In pastoral formation, the Seminary prepares seminarians to be shepherds in the image of Christ.[61] Church history is filled with accounts of pastoral ministry in a wide variety of settings: the first Christian missionaries preaching the Gospel to the pagan world, Peter Canisius restoring Catholicism in southern Germany in the

---

[58] Ibid., no. 153.
[59] Ibid., no. 94.

[60] Ibid., no. 113.
[61] Ibid., no. 119.

Reformation era, Benedict XV striving to alleviate suffering in the First World War, and the future John Paul II struggling for religious freedom in Communist Poland.

At one seminary where I taught previously, the school identified thirty-five learning outcomes for graduates of the MDiv program. Fifteen of these were addressed in my courses. While most were in the area of intellectual formation, church history significantly contributed to other dimensions as well.

Eight of the listed intellectual outcomes were addressed in church history. Besides the ability to understand and to articulate Roman Catholic Church History in the time periods being studied, these included:

- To demonstrate adequate understanding of major theological themes in the Christian, and in particular Roman Catholic tradition.
- To understand and be able to articulate the Christian Tradition in the areas in which the student has studied.
- To be able to use contemporary theological research methods in order to interpret principal theological sources and to be able to do advanced theological research.
- To be competent in employing appropriate resources for serious theological research and to be able to apply it to one's ministry.

- To demonstrate an openness for on-going intellectual development and theological reflection.
- To be able to apply the Christian tradition to modern issues and problems.
- To demonstrate an appreciation for the connection between the study and teaching of theology and the call to serve the church and the world.

Three human formation objectives were also addressed in these courses. These included:

- To understand the need for openness to ongoing growth and development.
- To appreciate the importance of the human side of ministry and the need to relate to effectively and appropriately to others.
- To appreciate the need to develop the capacity for sound prudential judgment.

Church history is also good for discernment. If seminarians wonder whether they are worthy of living up to their vocation, they can see the struggles and human limitations of past church leaders.

Spiritual formation objectives in church history included:

- To understand the history of the spiritual tradition of the Church in such a way as to be able to nurture and sustain a commitment to ongoing conversion and a deep personal relationship with the Triune God.

- To understand the Christian spiritual tradition.

Finally, there were two pastoral formation objectives as well:

- To study collaborative leaders of the past who called forth the gifts of all and who worked to resolve conflicts justly.
- To study servant leaders of the past who ministered in various settings and for diverse constituencies; and with and within multi-cultural settings.

## Models of Church History

There are various theological models that can be employed in teaching Catholic history. These are not only helpful in understanding the past, but can also help future priests envision how the Christian community engages the world. The first is the Pentecost model. This sees the Church as a community of ordinary people who, with the Holy Spirit, can achieve extraordinary things.

The next is the Incarnation model, making sure that the human side of the Church is not overshadowed by the divine side, but presented in an integrated way. This intentionally adds flesh and blood to the story to prevent a drift into excessive hagiography. This "warts and all" approach should be complemented with a sound theology of sin, which will be addressed below.

Then there is the City of God model. The Church is in the world, but not of the world. Church history is the story of the Christian community on its pilgrimage from this world to the next. While on this pilgrimage, it does not renounce the world but engages it by preaching the Good News and promoting the common good until it retires from its labors and arrives at its true home, the Heavenly Jerusalem.

The Second Vatican Council's Dogmatic Constitution on Divine Revelation provides another model for understanding a human church which is divinely inspired. Just as the Holy Spirit inspired the human author of the Sacred Scriptures, so the Spirit also inspires the Church. We are the paper upon which the Holy Spirit writes the history of the Church. So, like Sacred Scripture, we need to understand the culture, times, and people of the past to discern the message to be gleaned from Church's journey through history.

## Catholic History and Theodicy

Finally, when teaching Catholic history in any pastoral ministry program, I believe it is important to have a good theology of evil. If we shield students from the uncomfortable parts of the Church's past, passing over when people acting in the Church's name have sinned, then church history is reduced to hagiography and simply recounts the stories of the saints. This does not serve future church leaders well, leaving them unprepared for the human side of the Church, as we have seen in the pedophilia scandal. A good theology of evil can also help prevent the opposite problem, that of dwelling excessively on these evils and becoming cynical.

The Lisbon Earthquake of 1755 is an example of why this is necessary. On All Saints Day, 1755 Lisbon was hit by a 9.0 earthquake, followed by a fire and a tsunami. Eighty-five percent of the of city was destroyed, with a death toll of 40,000 or 20% of the population. A great loss of faith followed this disaster as people asked how could God have allowed this to happen. The Holocaust, the pedophilia crisis, and the loss of loved ones to terminal illness are modern examples.

Church history needs to be more than hagiography. It is true that the history of the Church is full of truly holy, inspiring people. Still, we must not neglect the sins of the Church. It is interesting to note that the Church itself tacitly recognizes that it was in need of reform in the 16th century by the fact that there is an over 250-year gap in canonized popes until Pope Pius V and the reforms of the Counter-Reformation. An awareness of the sins of our faith community can also put us on guard against those wolves in sheep's clothing who would take advantage of the good name of the Church, earned at a great price by the saints and martyrs, for their own purposes.

Any valid theodicy must balance three points. First, that evil does exist. Secondly, that the omnipotent, omniscient, and omnibenevolent God is offended by sin. Thirdly, that the human person possesses genuine freedom and moral responsibility. Two classic Christian theodicies in

addressing evil are those of Irenaeus of Lyons and Augustine of Hippo.

Irenaeus (d. 202 AD) taught that creation has two stages: In the first, humans were created in the image of God and will later be shaped in the likeness of God. Humans are imperfect because the second stage is incomplete. To achieve this likeness of God, humans must continue to develop. Irenaeus argued that evil and suffering exists in the world because this is the best way for humans to develop. God allows evil for the moral education of people.

Irenaeus further asserted that the created world is the best of all possible worlds because it allows humans to fully develop. A world containing evil and suffering would allow development better than one which does not.

Origen (d. 253 AD) taught a similar theodicy. He described the world as a school or hospital for souls. Suffering plays both an educative and healing role, with God acting as both Teacher and Physician.

The other classic theodicy, that of Augustine of Hippo (d. 430 AD), is a response to the concern that if God is omnipotent and omnibenevolent, then there should be no evil in the world. Having rejected the dualistic Manichean belief that good is the creation of one divine being, and

> **"The Church is composed of both saints and sinners, struggling forward in their earthly pilgrimage sustained by God's grace."**

evil by another, Augustine asserted that all creation is by the one God. The Augustinian theodicy asserts that God created the world *ex nihilo*, but maintains that God did not create evil and is not responsible for its occurrence. God is good and everything created is good. Evil as a substance does not exist, but it is rather the absence of good. Just as darkness is the absence of light and cold the absence of heat, so evil is the absence of good.

One of the greatest goods God created was free will, which human beings misused to sin. The free will of humans is offered by the Augustinian theodicy as the continued reason for moral evil. Another key element of this theodicy is Original Sin. It is the one exception to the humanity that Jesus shares with us. Sin is part of what it means to be human, so it should not come as a shock when it is encountered in church history.

We see Augustine's theodicy in action in both the Donatist and Pelagian controversies. Donatism had serious ecclesiological implications, stressing that the Church could only be composed of the saints and that the sacraments of sinful clergy were invalid. Augustine provides us with the view that the Church is composed of both saints and sinners, which serves as a good theological model for church history. Likewise, with Pelagianism, Augustine stresses the reality of human sin and the need for grace. This too is

a good model for church history, the flawed People of God struggling forward in their earthly pilgrimage sustained by God's grace.

Again, the Irenaean and Augustinian theodicies are classic examples. A fruitful dialogue with colleagues in the moral and fundamental theology departments can lead to awareness of contemporary theodicies and their implications for church history.

## Conclusion

In conclusion, while there are unique elements in teaching Catholic history in pastoral ministry programs, such as theologies of evil, a preoccupation with ecclesiastical politics, etc., at the end of the day we are still teaching history. There needs to be critical thinking and relying on documentation in trying to grasp the past as we move into the future. An education drawing on such historical expertise will benefit students preparing for any career, including the priesthood.

Dr. Dennis Castillo, M.A., Ph.D. (dcastillo@stmarys.edu).
Doctor Castillo is Professor of Church History and Associate Dean of Assessment and Accreditation at St. Mary's Seminary & University.

# Teaching Marian Doctrine and Spirituality in a Catholic Seminary

## Dennis J. Billy, C.Ss.R., D.Min., Th.D., S.T.D.

### Introduction

Because Mary is both Mother of God and Mother of the Church, she should hold a prominent place in the curriculum of every Catholic seminary. Her place in seminary life should permeate every aspect of a seminarian's formation—the human, the spiritual, the intellectual, and the pastoral—and in such a way that these dimensions are themselves holistically integrated into seminary culture. Seminarians, in other words, need to know how she touches them personally, devotionally, doctrinally, and ministerially. They need to view Mary as Jesus' first and closest disciple, a safeguard for the purity of Church teaching, and a wellspring of personal and communal devotion.[1] Because she is Mother of God and Mother of the Church, Mary is also our mother. From these basic relationships, all else flows.

### Jesus' First and Closest Disciple

Mary was Jesus' first and closest disciple. She was with him at the moments of his conception and birth, throughout his hidden and public lives, and during his passion and death on the cross. According to tradition, she was also the first person Jesus appeared to after his resurrection from the dead.

> "Because Mary is both Mother of God and Mother of the Church, she should hold a prominent place in the curriculum of every Catholic seminary."

Since Jesus first saw the light of day when he emerged from the darkness of Mary's womb, it was fitting that he would appear to her first when he left his tomb and brought new light to our darkened world. (This explains why there was no need for her to go to the empty tomb—she already knew he had risen!) What is more, she now sits at his right hand and rules as Queen of the heaven and earth. Mary, as the Little Flower tells us, "is Queen of heaven and earth, but she is more Mother than Queen."[2] She watches over us with motherly care and affection and bids us to follow her as she denies herself and takes up her cross in the following of her Son. When seen in this light, Mary is the model of Christian discipleship. We

---

[1] For an extended development of these three Marian themes, see Dennis J. Billy, C.Ss.R., *Mary in 3-D: Icon of Discipleship, Doctrine, and Devotion* (Hyde Park, NY: New City Press, 2015).

[2] Thérèse of Lisieux, *St. Therese of Lisieux: Her Last Conversations*, trans. John Clarke, O.C.D. (Washington, D.C.: ICS Publications, 1977), 161.

look to her as one who embodies what it means to walk in the footsteps of the Lord.

The word, "disciple," is related to the word, "discipline." A disciple is someone who follows the way of a master. He or she seeks to assimilate not only the master's teachings but also the way he lives. Mary is the model of Christian discipleship, because she was present to her Son ever since the angel Gabriel announced to her that she was to conceive and bear a son by the power of the Holy Spirit. She herself was immaculately conceived so that, full of grace, she could provide a fitting dwelling place for the Lord when he entered our world. She stood close to him all through his earthly life and remains so even now as she intercedes us from heaven to make sure that her sons and daughters have all they need for a fruitful following of Christ. Mary's one and only desire is to draw others closer to her Son. Those who walk with Mary also walk with her Son. Their two hearts are so closely joined that friendship with one necessarily includes friendship with the other. Whenever we gather in Jesus' name, Mary, the humble handmaiden and servant of the Lord, is not very far away. Her closeness to her Son comes before our closeness to her children. As Pope Francis once said, "We Christians are not orphans, we have a mama, we have a mother, and this is great! We are not orphans! The Church is mother, Mary is mother."[3]

Mary reflects in her life the essential qualities of authentic discipleship. First and foremost, she is a *faithful* disciple, someone who trusts in the Lord with her whole heart mind, soul, and strength. She *loves* the Lord so much that she is willing to follow him wherever he goes, even if it means giving up her life for his sake. What is more, she is also a *servant* of the Lord. She looks upon herself as someone who seeks to do whatever the Lord asks of her. She does not shy away from difficult tasks and yet is completely happy with doing the menial tasks of daily life, such as housekeeping, cooking, laundry, and the like. She finds fulfilment, moreover, *doing the Lord's will*, her will is one with the will of her Son. The two are so closely intertwined that it is difficult to tell them apart. Her life is also filled with *joy*. Joy is one of the fruits of the Spirit and Mary was (and is) someone filled with the Spirit. Her humble *Magnificat* is a great hymn of Christian joy. She embodies the words of St. Paul in his letter to the Philippians:

> "Mary reflects in her life the essential qualities of authentic discipleship: faithfulness, service, and joy."

"Rejoice always, pray without ceasing, give thanks in all circumstances" (1 Th 5:16-18).[4] Mary finds joy in all who love her Son and seek to love as he loves. Those who do so are *beloved*

---

[3] Pope Francis, "General Audience (St. Peter's Square, September 3, 2014), https://www.vatican.va/content/francesco/en/audiences/2014/documents/papa-francesco_20140903_udienza-generale.html.

[4] All Scripture quotations come from *Holy Bible: New Revised Standard Version with Apocrypha* (New York: Oxford University Press,1989).

*by God* and by she who carried him in her womb and gave him life. As such, she is the mother of all Christian disciples.

## Model of Doctrinal Purity

In addition to being Jesus' first and closest disciple, Mary has also placed herself at the service of the Church as a way of defending its doctrinal integrity. When speaking with the Archangel Gabriel, she referred to herself as "the servant of the Lord" (Lk 1:38). That is to say that she has placed herself in the service of the Lord and his Church, the Mystical Body of Christ. To this end, the Church has often used her as a way of deepening our understanding of the mystery of Christ. When seen in this light, she has been used as a theological model to insure that the Church's proclamation of Christ has been kept theologically pure and free from error.

Mary, we might say, is both virgin and mother. As mother of the Church, she provides the faithful with a sense of warmth and belonging. We find ourselves at home in the Church, because Mary lives at its heart and makes it her home and our home. As a virgin, she serves the Church by being the means through which the Church was (and is) able to unlock for believers the mysteries of the faith. For example, at the Council of Ephesus in 431, she was proclaimed the Mother of God (*Theotokos*) in order to offset the erroneous Nestorian claim that she was the mother of Jesus (*Christotokos*) but not the Mother of God. Mary has been used in similar ways to help define other mysteries of the Catholic faith. She has been used by the Church in this way to explain, among other things, the doctrines of the virgin birth, her divine maternity, her Assumption into heaven, and her role as Intercessor and Mediatrix. As the "servant of the Lord," she has placed herself at the service of the Church for the sake of maintaining its doctrinal purity. When teaching Catholic seminarians, it is important to emphasize not only Mary as the mother of all disciples, but also the role she has played over the centuries in helping to maintain the integrity of the faith.

> **"Mary has been used as a theological model to ensure that the Church's proclamation of Christ has remained theologically pure and free from error."**

Mary's virginal purity, in other words, has been used as a means for the Church to safeguard the teachings of Christ and his Church. She does so by placing herself freely and willingly at the service of the Church who, since then, has used her as a theological model to maintain the unique balance between the human and divine present in Christ and his Church. As such, she truly is both Mother of God and Mother of the Church. These two roles cannot in no way be separated. To do so would be to dilute the great mystery of what God has given us in the Person of his Son, Jesus Christ, and the body of believers he has left behind. Some two thousand years ago, Mary conceived Jesus in her womb by the power of the Holy Spirit. Since then, the Spirit has continued to place her at the service of her Son and his Mystical Body. Mary, in other words, not only bore the Christ child in her womb to make possible the mystery of the Incarnation, but also carries within her Immaculate Heart God's pilgrim church on earth as she makes her way to the Kingdom which, at one and the same time, is already present, but still in come when the New Creation will manifest itself fully in the time to come.

## Mother of Devotion

In addition to being Jesus' first and closest disciple and someone who allows the Church to use her as an instrument for safeguarding its doctrinal integrity, Mary is also the Mother of Devotion. This role has two dimensions. We must not only consider Mary's devotion to her Son, but also our devotion to her on account of her unique role in the work of Redemption. Both of these, moreover, have both personal and communal aspects to them.

Mary was a devoted mother to her Son. She loved him will all her heart, mind, and soul. She cared for him in his infancy and raised him through his childhood and young adulthood. When his hidden life in Nazareth came to an end, she followed him throughout his public ministry, and stood by him all through his passion and death. What is more, she experienced him in his resurrected, glorified body, and was present in the upper room when the Holy Spirit descended upon the apostle in tongues of fire. She presently sits at her Son's right hand as Queen of Heaven and guides the Church with her motherly heart

that is filled with the Spirit. Mary's devotion to her Son is an inspiration for all Christians of what it means to be a loyal disciple The bond of love between she and her Son is indissoluble, just as is the bond between her and the Church, her Son's Mystical Body.

Mary's personal devotion to her Son also implies a singular devotion to the Father and Holy Spirit. Because Jesus is the Second Person of the Blessed Trinity, his relationship within this intimate community of love spills over into his other relationships, not the least of which is the special one he shares with his mother. Mary's devotion to her Son, in other words, necessarily involves her unqualified devotion to the Trinity. Her humble fiat, "…let it be with me according to your word" (Lk 1: 38), was an act of loving obedience to the God of her Fathers, a God who though the words of the Angel Gabriel was already revealing to her something of the communal nature of his very existence. Her "Yes" to the Lord opened itself to the possibility that a transcendent God would overshadow her with his Spirit so that she could conceive and bring into the world the Only Begotten Son of the Father. When seen in this light, Mary's humble fiat was a "Yes" to the mystery of our transcendent, immanent, and incarnate God.

Mary's singular devotion to her Son and the Blessed Trinity has concrete implications for what our devotion to her should be like. One the one hand, each of us called to foster a deep devotion to her on a personal level. On the other hand, we are also asked to recognize her as a gift to the

Church at large, both local and universal and, for this reason, to nurture and sustain a communal devotion to her as the People of God. Mary, in other words, is Mother to us both as individuals and as a communal whole. She nurtures each of us in the faith spiritually and is Mother to us as the family of the Church, the community of believers in Christ Jesus, her Son. As we shall see, these two dimensions are themselves intimately related.

Just as each of us is called to foster in our lives a personal relationship with Jesus Christ, we are also called to do so with Mary, his Mother. Mary is Jesus' Mother and our Mother. Our relations with her should be one of filial loyalty and devotion. Just as our relationship with Jesus is fostered through our participation in Church life, the reception of the sacraments, and personal time spent with him in prayer, the same hold true for our relationship with Mary. As Mother of the Church, Mary is present in all Church worship. She is also present to us when we bring to her our needs and petitions, as we ask for her to intercede with her Son on our behalf. Because we are physical as well as psychological, spiritual, and social creatures, we need to have concrete ways of expressing our love and devotion to her. Simple prayers such as the Rosary, the Angelus, the Litany of Mary, and the Hail Holy Queen are traditional ways in which the faithful have down through the years fostered their relationship with Mary. It is also very helpful if we foster a

> **"Mary's devotion to her Son inspires the faithful to nurture a personal and communal relationship with the Blessed Mother."**

particular devotion to Mary under one of her many titles (e.g., Our Mother of Perpetual Help, Our Lady Seat of Wisdom, The Immaculate Heart of Mary, the Brown Scapular). These and other devotions go a long way in helping us to deepen our relationship with Our Blessed Mother.

Mary, however, is not only the Mother of each of us, but also the Mother of all of us. As such we are called as a community of believers to give her a special type of veneration (*hyperdulia*), which differs from the worship (*latria*), given to God alone, and the typical veneration (*dulia*) we render to the saints. When seen in this light, Catholics do not worship Mary, as some Protestants claim, but give her a special type of saintly veneration because of the important role she played in the mystery of our redemption and because she is the greatest of the saints and followers of her Son. For this reason, it is important that we celebrate her feasts (e.g., her Immaculate Conception, her glorious Assumption, Mary, her Motherhood of God, her Motherhood of the Church—to name but a few) with special reverence and devotion. It is important that we express our communal devotion to her through the celebration of her liturgical feasts, to be sure, but also through common novenas, processions, solidarities dedicated to Our Lady, and the like. What is more, it is also important for us to realize that our personal devotion to Mary is intimately connected to our communal devotional to her—and vice versa. Our personal devotion, in other words, should deepen our communal devotion, while the latter is likewise closely related to our private devotions. If this intimate link is in any way disturbed, a danger may arise that our devotion to Our Lady has somehow gone awry. This delicate balance must be maintained at all costs.

## In a Catholic Seminary

The question now arises: How can a Catholic seminary instill authentic Marian doctrine and spirituality in its students? The following remarks, while by no means exhaustive, offer a number of suggestions for making sure Catholic seminarians receive a sure foundation in this area.

*To begin with, the seminary curriculum must focus not merely on the doctrinal aspects regarding Mary, but also the equally important formational and devotional aspects.* Mary was Jesus' first and closest disciple, has been used as a means for safeguarding the Church's doctrinal integrity (especially regarding her Son), and is model of motherly devotion to her Son and the Church. For these reasons, a seminary curriculum should emphasize Mary's discipleship, her use by the Church as a theological model for clarifying the faith, and her deep devotion to her Son and his body, the Church as a model for all believers.

*What is more, these three aspects—Mary's discipleship, her servant role as a theological model, and her motherly devotion to Christ and his Church—should not be viewed in isolation from* one another but as intimately connected. To emphasize one to the exclusion of the others would do an injustice to the seminarian's education and to Mary herself. Like her Son, Mary is a mystery, a woman wrapped in silence, whose role in God's plan of redemption cannot, important as it is, be easily reduced to a few dogmatic statements. She is God's gift to the Church and should be treated in a comprehensive, holistic manner, not one that diminishes her place in the Church by minimalizing her role in God's plan for humanity.

> **"Marian doctrine and spirituality should be holistically integrated into every dimension of seminary formation—human, intellectual, spiritual, and pastoral."**

*Marian doctrine and spirituality, in other words, should not be treated in isolation from one another but as two essential aspects of the person chosen by God to actively participate in humanity's redemption.* Mary, the New Eve, is the mother of the New Creation. For this reason, we need to engage her as a person and relate to her on the many levels of her human makeup: the physical, psychological/intellectual, spiritual, and social. We need to avoid an abstract knowledge of her place in the Church and recognize that the Church's doctrinal teachings about her merely scratch the surface of who she is and what she is about. Like every human person, Mary is a mystery, created in the image and likeness of God. Because she is the Mother of God she is even more deeply emersed in the mystery of our salvation and should be revered as both Queen and Mother.

*The seminary curriculum, moreover, should encourage candidates for the priesthood to engage her on every dimension of their priestly formation: the human, intellectual, spiritual, and pastoral.* They should relate to Mary personally as their spiritual mother, respect her for her role in helping the Church clarify the truths of the faith regarding her Son and his body, the Church, turn to her regularly in heartfelt prayer with our various needs and petitions, and also carry with them in all they do, especially in their ministry to the people they are called to serve. Their approach to Mary should be one that seeks to integrate these various dimensions into their priestly lives. Not to do so runs the risk of reducing Mary to various role and stereotypes that do not do justice to her integrity as Mother of God and Mother of the Church.

*From a strictly doctrinal perspective, the Church's teaching on Mary is a point of convergence for many of its theological disciplines: Christian anthropology, Christology, Ecclesiology, Eschatology—to name but a few.* The study of the doctrines regarding her can be a way of integrating these various theological subdisciplines and preventing them from retreating into isolated silos. When seen in this light, Mariology (as it is called) can be a way of bringing all of these theological disciplines together. Doing so would enable seminarians to view Catholic theology as an integral whole rather than a series of isolated intellectual endeavors. The end result of such an approach would be a seminarian who view Mary not on the periphery of the Church's theological endeavors but at its very heart.

"*If you are a theologian, you will pray truly. And if you pray truly, you*

> "Mary is not peripheral to theology but stands at its very heart, drawing all theological disciplines into a unified vision of faith."

*are a theologian.*"[5] These words of Evagrius Ponticus (d. 399 AD) highlight the intimate relationship between theological reflection and a life of prayer. This insight holds true especially when teaching Marian doctrine and spirituality. Mary was someone whose intimate relationship with the Lord led her to pray *The Magnificat*, one of the most beautiful hymns of the Christian religion, one rife with profound theological insights into the mystery of God and his love for his people. In a similar way, seminarians should be encouraged to integrate their theological lives with their spiritual lives. The best way to communicate that value is if their professors themselves value the importance of this integration in their own lives and communicate that to their students in the classroom.

*Finally, teaching Marian doctrine and spirituality to Catholic seminarians should address the*

---

[5] Evagrius Ponticus, *On Prayer*, no. 61 in *The Philokalia: The Complete Text* eds. G.E. H. Palmer, Philip Sherard, and Kallistos Ware, vol. 1 (London: Faber and Faber, 1979), 62.

*whole person and take place not only in the classroom but also in every other aspect of seminary life: in chapel, at meals, during common recreation, on retreat days, and in pastoral service to others.* There is, in other words, both a Petrine and a Marian dimension in Catholic life, and seminarians need to be exposed to and rooted in both. If the former focuses on the institutional and administrative skills of Church leadership, the latter nourishes the compassionate dimensions of selfless love that all Christians are called to embody in their lives. Catholic seminary culture should foster each of these values in its everyday life. To do otherwise runs the creating priests with educated minds but stony hearts, leaders with highly honed administrative skills but without the capacity for empathy and active listening.

## Conclusion

Teaching Marian doctrine and spirituality in a Catholic seminary involves a number of inter-related activities. Professors, formators, and spiritual directors need to be aware that they must convey not only *knowledge about* but also *knowledge of* Mary is a holy person, the first among the saints in the kingdom of heaven. She is the Mother of God and the Mother of the Church. She sits at the right hand of her Son as Queen of heaven and looks upon her sons and daughters with motherly care and affection. She

seeks our spiritual well-being and intercedes for us. Professors, formators, and spiritual directors need to promote the importance of fostering a deep love and devotion of Our Blessed Mother. From that all else flows.

Mary was (and is) Jesus' first and closest disciple. She also has placed herself at the service of the Church and used as a means of clarifying the mystery of her Incarnate Son. Her loving devotion to her Son, moreover, bids us to strive for the same heartfelt devotion towards Jesus *and* his mother. St. Irenaeus of Lyons (c. 130-202 AD) once said, "The glory of God is man fully alive."[6] Mary is the epitome of someone fully alive with the love of God. She is so close to her Son that his will is her will and her will his. We look at Mary and see in her

> **"The primary responsibility for teaching Marian doctrine and spirituality in a Catholic seminary lies not with the professors, mentors, or spiritual directors, but with the seminarians themselves."**

the vision that God has for us: to be fully alive with the love of God reigning in our hearts. That is why she is "our life, our sweetness, and our hope." The Catholic seminary is the place par excellence where this hope must be carefully tended in the mind and heart of each seminarian.

---

[6] Irenaeus of Lyons, *Against the Heresies*, 4.20.7 (CCC, no. 294).

In the final analysis, the primary responsibility for teaching Marian doctrine and spirituality in a Catholic seminary lies not with the professors, mentors, or spiritual directors, but with the seminarians themselves. It is their responsibility not only to learn everything they can about Mary, but also foster in their lives a deep personal love and devotion toward her. Failure to do so will impoverish their love for Christ and his Church. For this reason, they should strive to be close to the person Jesus was closest to during his earthly sojourn, who gave her to us as his parting gift from the cross (Jn 19:26-27), and with whom he remains so intimately close to this very day.

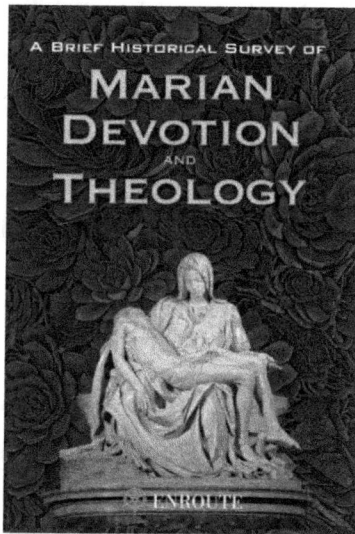

Dennis J. Billy, C.Ss.R., D.Min., Th.D., S.T.D. (dbilly@stmarys.edu)

Father Billy holds The Robert F. Leavitt Distinguished Service Chair in Theology and is Professor of Moral Theology and Spirituality at St. Mary's Seminary & University.

# Book Review: Tony's 50,000 Co-Incidence Miracles

**By Tony Coscia**
**Reviewed by Sebastian Mahfood, OP**

Late-vocation seminarians often describe being called into the priesthood by God due to some event or private revelation. Tony Coscia's story, which he tells in a book entitled *Tony's 50,000 Coincidence Miracles* (En Route Books & Media, 2017), resonates with many revelations. Those who notice God's voice in their lives know that they are being called into a more intentional engagement of their Christian faith. Some discern the call for priestly ministry while others discern it for lay ministries. Tony believes that the path Jesus called him to follow is a lay ministry of proclaiming the kingdom of God and evangelizing about the miracles Jesus performs daily in the life of each person.

Tony's story begins at a time in his life when he was feeling overwhelmed by various challenges, including financial difficulties and a lack of time for family. When he felt he had nowhere else to turn, he started having dreams about heaven and about feeling loved by God. He began reading the Bible and discovered that God had patience with even those who behaved poorly. His dreams of God's grace accompanied by his reading, then, led him into a desire to better understand his relationship with Jesus Christ. He began to wonder if he was truly hearing God's voice as evidenced by the miracles, or if the miracles were simply coincidences that he just happened to start noticing.

In a narrative that describes a hundred instances of divine intervention, guidance, and miracles in his life, especially those surrounding his wife, Julie's, death and the resolution of the financial difficulties that had long plagued him, Tony explains his method (the fleecing procedure) described in Judges 6:36-37. In those passages, the biblical author explains how Gideon seeks to discover if the calling he hears is truly from God by asking God for a sign. The New American Bible translates Gideon's pleading request in this way:

> "If indeed you are going to save Israel through me, as you have said, I am putting this woolen fleece on the threshing floor, and if [morning] dew is on the fleece alone, while all the ground is dry, I shall know that you will save Israel through me, as you have said."

This was an inspiration to Tony, who found his own fleecing method among the tools with which he was familiar in his accounting career – numbers – and describes his particular process for discerning the spirits, a process that has worked for him for over fifty years. In a similar way, he explains, that this process, which may be found both in his book and in his WCAT Radio podcasts really works for everyone.

Thus, Tony's message is a simple one – follow the promptings of Jesus Christ in your life once you discern they are truly from him. In Tony's case, he has catalogued at least three coincidence miracles a day for fifty years, sharing through his narratives how he's recognized over 50,000 of them. He came to the conclusion that others could use Gideon's method to strengthen their relationship with God in their lives, and he shares that amazingly true insight with everyone.

In addition to writing his books, Tony developed an email campaign, a radio ministry, and – most engaging of all – a business-card distribution ministry that enables him to approach people with a card and say, "Do you have a minute to hear about my book? About the miracles I've seen." His books give him a reason to walk up to anyone to share spiritual insights. To date, he's distributed over 10,000 business cards, which means that he's shared a personal witness story with that many people, in shopping malls, in parking lots, and on the beaches of southern Connecticut.

If Tony's message has an impact on our world, it will be in inspiring people to more intentionally reflect on their relationship with God and to seek to follow his will throughout their lives, which is not a small contribution for an evangelist to make in today's world.

For more on Tony's life and work, visit him online at https://wcatradio.com/miracles/

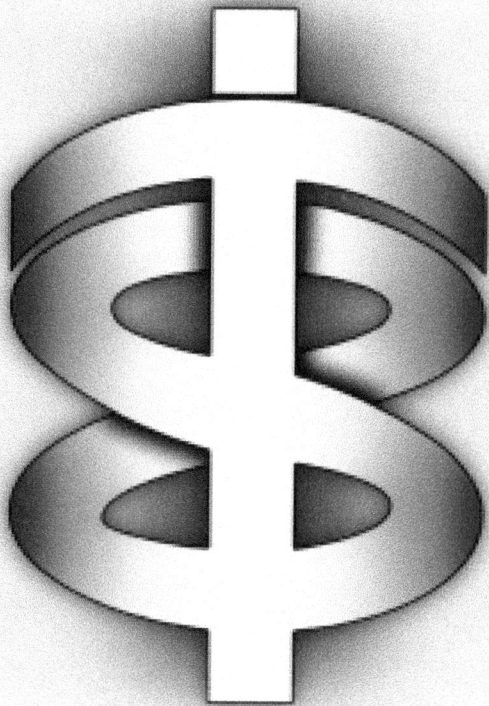

www.ingramcontent.com/pod-product-compliance
Lightning Source LLC
Chambersburg PA
CBHW081633040426

42449CB00014B/3290